ONE GOD, ONE MAN

Preludes to Scriptures

Jack Boyd

Printed in the United States of America.
Illustrations, Mark McCord
Typesetting and Book Design, Mel Ristau/Design

Library of Congress Card Number 87-72299
ACU Press, Abilene, Texas
ISBN - 0-915547-98-8   12345678

This one's for Joann

Preface

Many of us can recall a very special experience in our life when we had an encounter with our God that left us forever changed. It may have been the beginning of a completely new way of life that brought forgiveness, healing and an exciting intimacy with the Father that we had never imagined. That eventful day will remain in our memory forever as a precious treasure.

This poignantly illustrated book depicts that one special day in the lives of twelve men of the Bible when God became real to them and changed their lives.

Presented in the simple eloquence of a storyteller, each situation remains faithful to the text while it is re-created as it might have been. Each detail is well-researched and sensitive to the feelings and thoughts of each man as he encounters his God.

These stories may well bring a tear to your eye. Most certainly they will bring the warmth of love to your heart, love for God and love for all those who love Him.

Reading these stories will enhance your perception of the humanity of the heroes for the Bible as you empathize with their frustrations, participate in their struggles, and rejoice in their victories.

Bring you family together. Read and discuss these stories. Share the joy of trust in God.

Carl Brecheen
Abilene, Texas

Contents

1 Eliezer of the Caves

2 The Swordmaker

3 Elam the Traveler

4 The Jailkeeper

5 The Official from the Upper Nile

6 The Royal Official's Dying Son

7 The Final Gift

8 Matthias, The Nobody

9 The Old Warrior

10 The Messenger

11 The Man Born Blind

12 The Maker of Songs

ELIEZER OF THE CAVES

Eliezer leaned wearily against the wall of his cave, this tomb that was no longer used for dead people. He clenched, then stretched his fingers. "Perhaps today will be the day," he muttered, "the day when I hear the sound of a man speaking." He listened to the echo of his words far back in the cave. He turned and shouted angrily at the dark, dank hollow, "I want to speak words to another man, and then watch him smile and see him answer." He moved into the sunlight filtering through the fat juniper by his cave entrance. "Possibly they will leave me alone today. If I can just be alone, I know I can think of some escape." But he knew each time his mind began searching through his memories for answers... The Voices came back.

He was not old. He was not young. To be either of these there was a need for some comparison, some benchmark that would say, "Compared to the other olive growers in our village, Eliezer is still young," or "Eliezer is not as ancient as Old Penuel who lives near the well." But such a comparison required someone watching, someone nearby. For Eliezer there was no one for comparison. No one came near him. Ever. Not since The Voices.

He glanced around the fetid, musky cave. Despair covered his hunched shoulders like a shroud as he gazed at the few pitiful castoffs he kept so carefully arranged along the jagged walls. He knew they were almost useless, these bits and pieces from the warmth of human society, but they were all he could find to remind him of his village where his parents and his two sisters lived. He tried to remember how it felt to sit in a house and speak to someone.

His finger traced the broken handle of a small clay vase near his side. Would his baby sister like it? He forced his voice into what he remembered as a kind sound. "Here, young sister, is a vase I bought in the market today." No, he thought, I should speak with more gentleness. "Here, young sister, is a... " His head shook sadly. His sister was no longer young. She might even be married. At least a dozen years, no, more than that, had passed since the villagers drove him to this place. Then the tears began. What is the use, he thought morosely, of practicing my speaking when I will never see her or my mother or father or even a villager again. His head tilted back as the sobs gradually died. He picked up the cheap vase. Who else had touched it, he wondered? After all these years, could there be a small bit of the maker's or the owner's life still attached to the earthcolored container? A tiny dented brass cup, probably the plaything of a rich man's child, glistened in a stray patch of sun. He was reaching to pick it up when a movement not far from the shore of the sea caught his attention.

He squinted into the sunlight, his excitement building. Fishermen, he wondered? He leaped through the cave opening into the shadow of the huge juniper guarding this hole in the side of his hill. Several men sat in a large boat as three men jumped into the water to tug it onto the stony beach. Eliezer frowned. Why here, he wondered? Fishermen land farther down the beach where the water is deeper. On the other hand, no other people came by boat to this rocky hill country. He edged cautiously through the shade of the squat, aromatic shrub so his movements would not be noticed. There was something odd about the people still in the boat. They all gazed at a man near the bow, but that man was saying nothing.

Suddenly, as if by a giant fist, Eliezer was knocked to the ground. No! he thought. Not now! Not here with strangers who would not know him and would not run from him. Please, he begged. Please!

"Stop looking at that man," The Voices within Eliezer rasped." If you think we have hurt you, then do not go near that one in the boat. He will do worse!"

Eliezer had to get away before they tormented him more. His muscles bulged as he tried desperately to pull himself erect, but with each effort something, someone kicked the rocks away or loosened the scrub bush his bleeding fingers grasped. He flopped around like some giant, smelly fish as The Voices echoed in his ears: "Do you like torture? Then go speak to that one who is their leader. You will learn about pain as never before."

"But I only want to hear what they . . . "

"Never!" a bass voice snarled. The sound was like a tree splitting, or the echo of lightning. "You live for us. You cannot talk with anyone, ever!

"But I will only listen!"

"Can you not hear?" another Voice squeaked. It was the sound of an animal caught in a trap. "We only do this!" Eliezer felt himself scrubbed around the stony hillside as if dragged by a huge hand. "That one will surely kill you." The voice dropped to a malevolent whisper. "We only play!"

Carefully, painfully Eliezer rolled into a sitting position. Without noticing it, he wiped some blood from his arm. Such a small cut was beneath notice when compared with the other bruises and scars he carried. No, he thought, there is no reason to go down there. They're not even carrying a basket for food. There was no reason to frighten them. He began scooting crab-like back up the hill, pulling himself with scratched hands into the protective shade of the old juniper. The Voices he feared and hated subsided into a tiny whine in his ears which he could not understand.

He stretched to ease the fire in his lacerated shoulders as he crawled through the narrow entrance into his cave. He tried to stand, but the pain of seeing another human so close without talking to him was more than he could bear. Eliezer collapsed onto the small fragment of carpet he kept near one wall. It was old and musty, but since it stayed in the dark cave the colors were only partially faded, and it had become one of his prized possessions. He spread it directly beneath the small gouged-out space in the dusty wall which held the metal bands and chains.

His gaze lifted toward the pile of rough iron. Tentatively he touched one of the leg irons. He remembered when the men from the village surprised him one stormy night. Many men, eight, twelve, he didn't know, jumped on him and pressed the iron bands around his ankles until a clamp snapped into place. He remembered the grotesque shadows dancing across the cave wall while the men jeered and threw lumps of dirt at him.

That was when The Voices, angry and jealous, came boiling up from within him. It was as if a typhoon raged out of his mouth. The men's faces changed from laughter to terror as they stumbled backward. He took one step and felt the iron chain clank at its limit. Then, with The Voices screaming obscenities through his mouth, his feet began a maniacal dance. Suddenly, his body convulsed violently. He kicked and the iron chain snapped with a sound like a guard's whip. The village men screamed as they clawed their way out of the cave and lurched down the hill.

From that time he kept the various pieces of iron in the niche in the wall. He didn't exactly pray to them; they just formed a point of reference for his pain. They were heavy, they were rusted in places, and they reminded him of his years in this cave, the years since he was a small boy and The Voices came to him while he still lived in the village. In an odd way they brought to his memory the people in the village, his village, the one he was forbidden to see or visit.

He wept silently as he crawled toward the mouth of his cave. "When will I die," his pleading voice asked the silences. "I have tried to kill myself, but The Voices only let me bleed and hurt. They keep me as a plaything, as I keep the rug and the dented brass cup and the leg irons." The sun's warmth caressed his lacerated back as he pulled himself through the opening. Then he saw the man, the leader from the boat. The man sat on a rock talking to his companions as if he were teaching them something. But as he talked he looked upward. Eliezer saw he was looking toward this cave!

Eliezer knew he had been seen, but instead of fright there was only a tiny smile of... what?... of welcome?... on the man's face. Although far away, Eliezer saw this teacher was not afraid. It was as if... as if... he sat waiting for Eliezer.

"He says he is the Son of the Most High God!" The keening whine of one of The Voices blistered Eliezer's ears with its scream.

The teacher on the rock stood and turned toward him.

"He will torture you!" two voices squealed like dying animals.

The teacher nodded without moving.

With The Voices screaming obscenities through his mouth, Eliezer rolled from the cave to plunge down the stone-littered hill toward the man. The teacher's companions scrambled for the safety of the boat. The teacher only held out his hand.

The Voices tripped Eliezer, but he scrambled to his feet. They grabbed for his cloak, but he shrugged out of it and ran on naked. Their bellowing screeched like a whirlwind through a thousand caves. Then, without warning, they stopped.

Eliezer staggered to a halt. He waited for the falling and the cutting and the screaming... but it never started. He waited for the teacher to run as all the rest did. But the man only held out his hand. Eliezer touched his ears, then snapped his fingers to see if his hearing was gone. He heard only the sound of the lapping waves and the sighing wind. He was naked, but the teacher seemed not to mind.

His eyes widened as if awakening from a dream. Or was this the taunting nightmare? Would the teacher cry out at the last minute and run as the dozens and hundreds always did before? No, he stood as if waiting for a friend, a small smile on his lips, nodding slowly to encourage Eliezer.

Would this be the day he touched another human after so many years? Tears washed dusty rivulets on Eliezer's scarred cheeks as he walked toward the outstretched arms.

They went across the lake to the region of the Gerasenes. When Jesus got out of the boat, a man with an evil spirit came from the tombs to meet him. This man lived in the tombs, and no one could bind him any more, not even with a chain. For he had often been chained hand and foot, but he tore the chains apart and broke the irons on his feet. No one was strong enough to subdue him. Night and day among the tombs and in the hills he would cry out and cut himself with stones.

When he saw Jesus from a distance, he ran and fell on his knees in front of him. He shouted at the top of his voice, "What do you want with me, Jesus, Son of the Most High God? Swear to God that you won't torture me!" For Jesus was saying to him, "Come out of this man, you evil spirit!"

Then Jesus asked him, "What is your name?"

"My name is Legion," he replied, "for we are many." And he begged Jesus again and again not to send them out of the area.

A large herd of pigs was feeding on the nearby hillside. The demons begged Jesus, "Send us among the pigs; allow us to go into them." He gave them permission, and the evil spirits came out and went into the pigs. The herd, about two thousand in number, rushed down the steep bank into the lake and were drowned.

Those tending the pigs ran off and reported this in the town and countryside, and the people went out to see what had happened. When they came to Jesus, they saw the man who had been possessed by the legion of demons, sitting there, dressed and in his right mind; and they were afraid. Those who had seen it told the people what had happened to the demonpossessed man—and told about the pigs as well. Then the people began to plead with Jesus to leave their region.

As Jesus was getting into the boat, the man who had been demonpossessed begged to go with him. Jesus did not let him, but said, "Go home to your family and tell them how much the Lord has done for you, and how he has had mercy on you." So the man went away and began to tell in the Decapolis how much Jesus had done for him. And all the people were amazed.

Mark 5:1-20 [NIV]

THE
SWORDMAKER

2

"Hud! Get in here!"

The young man, his face glistening from hammering the glowing iron bar, frowned toward the dim storage room and his father's rasping shout.

"If I leave this sword," Hud said carefully, "it will cool and I will never be able to finish it today." He turned just in time to see his father shove through the rough door of the storage room. The older man, broad shouldered from a lifetime of swinging a metal mallet on red-hot iron, held a short, slightly curved sword in his thick fist.

"Hud, what is this?" It was obviously a statement, not a question.

Hud quickly dropped the metal rod he had been hammering back on the glowing coals of the forge. With a jerked wave of his hand he motioned his father back into the storage room. "Father... you know it's mine." Hud stood straight, his dark eyes and square face refusing to quail before his father's anger. A lifetime spent enduring the taunts of his four brothers and the neighborhood boys echoed in his memory. He pulled his left arm behind his back so his father couldn't see him flex his left hand.

"Ehud," the old man said slowly and carefully, as if teaching a child a new word, "tell me what is wrong with this sword."

"Nothing," the young man said softly. "It's perfect. But, the sword is for me, and... therefore... it's lefthanded." Hud reached for the bright metal object, but Gera pulled it back.

"Are we so rich that we can afford time at the forge to make playthings?" Old Gera pulled in a deep breath as he looked down at the short, curved sword. In disgust he threw it on a table. "Hud, we cannot take the chance of making the Captain of the King's Armor angry." Gera swung back toward his son. "Hide it. Bury it! It could get us killed. Then, get clean. The day is over. I must eat quickly and go to the Elders' Group."

Hud twisted and in three quick steps caught up with his father. "You tell me about getting killed, and then you go to your illegal meeting!"

Gera lifted his hand to strike his son, but something in the boy's eyes stopped the hand from falling. No, Gera thought, he's still young, and besides, he's lefthanded, so what could I teach such a boy. He shook his head at the injustice that, besides living in a conquered country, he should be given the burden of a defective son. "Just bury that toy. Then get ready to eat."

Ehud gazed at the perfectly formed sword with its etched hand guard. For many months he worked secretly to make this the finest sword to come from the forge of Gera. The two edges were as sharp as any fine razor, and the double groovings down each side were perfect. And his father knew it! Old Gera had an eye for sword making that outdid any other iron worker in the country. Oh, yes, his father knew! Hud carefully rewrapped the sword and hid it in the shallow hole in the dirt floor. Then he walked next door to his home.

The four brothers and two sisters of Hud, all but one older than he, came in and gathered up pieces of bread and small bowls of fragrant meat broth. They sat against the walls of the earthen house on tiny pieces of worn carpeting, talking about people they had seen, pieces of metal they worked, gossip of the village. Twice Hud tried to break into the conversation, but each time they ignored him. Once his younger brother said something about making a lefthanded bowl for him. The older brothers smiled at the little family joke. Hud got up slowly and carried his food up to his favorite place, the small balcony on top of their house. Twilight faded under a line of clouds as up in the hills he watched tiny lights flare and others wink out. He wondered if there were others who were like him, who used their left hand for...

He stretched his tired muscles. Although the smallest of the five sons of Gera, and still with only a scraggly beard, he was as strong as any of them. In wrestling matches on festival days he could best any man in the village, although the losers muttered that he stood with the wrong foot forward. He frowned up at the approaching dark purple of the night sky. Then the image of the curved sword flashed through his mind, and he smiled.

Hud was born three years before Eglon, the Tri-King, formed the Confederacy of the Three and attacked Hud's small country. As a child Hud heard the legends of the invincible men who used Gera's fine swords. As a child he often picked up the large broad-bladed swords and swung them around his head, but the hand guards were wrong. His right hand just could not grasp the handles properly, and there were no left-handed swords ordered by the Sword Captain. None, that is, until two years before when the idea for the bright, short sword first started as a dim idea in Hud's mind.

Suddenly a scratching sound in the twisting alley behind their house caused him to turn. His father almost ran around the fence and into the back door of their house, his movement betraying his agitated mind. "Hud." His father's voice was strangely excited. "Hud! Are you on the roof?"

The young man jumped down the ladder two rungs at a time, then stood peering into his father's restless, bright eyes.

"The rest of you, sit. Hud, stand here next to me." Quickly, like milling ants in a disturbed hill, the four brothers, two sisters and the mother sat, their faces mixed with fear and excitement. "You know I've been with the Elder's Group of this village. And, an amazing thing... an unbelievable thing... has happened!" He stroked his beard, his habit when he was agitated. "We, that is, they have decided that now is the time for our country to overthrow King Eglon." The brothers started to get up, but Gera motioned them back down with a nervous wave. "Stay where you are. I have to give you the words of the Elders." Gera hesitated, almost fearful at the words to come. "The one who goes first against Eglon... is Ehud."

Hud wondered if his ears were playing tricks. "Is this from the Elders?"

"Not entirely," Gera said carefully, as if recounting words he heard somewhere else. "The Prophet from the City of Palms was here tonight. He said that our village was chosen to provide the—leader—for our revolt. He said he had been told such a man would come from here, and... "

"And—Hud is to go first?" It was the eldest of the brothers speaking. "Was that the message?" Disbelief and anger mixed in his voice.

"The Elders tested it. The Prophet brought us the message, and we made the test. We stood in a circle, and I brought my small knife, the one that is perfectly balanced." Old Gera raised his head to gaze at the flickering lamp as if seeing beyond it to another time. "The Prophet spun the knife, and it stopped with the point toward me. The Elders wanted another trial. Again it stopped pointing directly at me. Then they accepted it."

"But a lefthanded leader?" It was the youngest brother. "None of our legends tell of a simpleminded leader!"

Old Gera turned sharply. "It was a fair test. The Prophet said it would come from my household, so he spun the knife again and again to choose which of my five sons would serve. The knife always indicated Hud."

The brothers all stood, their voices a confused babble. "A lefthanded leader!... an idiot savior... the village will never allow... "

"Stop!" Old Gera pushed through the arguing brothers. "The Elders have chosen. Hud will be the one."

The eldest brother walked insolently to Hud and looked down at him. "And just how is Hud to save us?"

Old Gera stood silent for many seconds. He glanced at his wife, huddled in the corner, fear covering her like a blanket. "Hud is to kill Eglon."

The preposterous sound of the words silenced everyone. It was as if someone had been asked to gather a star, or to pull smoke back in a chimney. Hud, the imbecile, the non-leader, the lefthanded? Absurd! "How will we know for sure that he is the chosen one?" another brother asked.

Old Gera was not able to lift his head. "When he returns alive," he said in a half-whisper.

Hud was too shocked to react. Then, in the space of a blinking eye, he felt a clean wind blow through his mind, sharpening images and aiming his thoughts. He turned to his father. "I will not be alone on my walk. You know this, Father."

Old Gera turned slowly, as if hearing from a great distance. He, too, saw something new, something that had been there all the time, but fog-covered. Suddenly, with a rush, he realized he had placed the fog there himself. He assumed the folk tales of the village were true, that to use the other hand was wrong. Now, he thought back to the months and years of working the forge, and always Hud was the one who understood first, the one who rough-sketched the best new designs, the one the Captain of the Armory always sought out. Old Gera closed his eyes at his memories. I knew, he thought, all the time I knew!

"It is as you said, my son, you will not be alone on your walk. Do you know what you will do?"

Ehud, his heart pounding, walked across the room and gazed out the door at the night sky. "Father, what is different about me?" He turned quickly. "No, you don't have to answer, because we all know. Then, what will help me when I go on the Prophet's mission? It will be the one thing that kept me from doing the predictable, that prevented my mind from working in the normal channels." He walked to his father. "The one who has chosen me has chosen for my difference." He paused. "When do I leave?"

Old Gera placed his hands on his son like a benediction. "Tonight," he said simply.

Ehud looked out at the night sky. Without a word,
he turned and walked out the door. He returned with the
bright, curved, short sword. He looked at his brothers, his
sisters, then at his weeping mother. Finally, he turned to his
father. "Is it time?"

"Yes. Time."

---

*Again the Israelites cried out to the Lord, and he
gave them a deliverer—Ehud, a left-handed man, the son of
Gera the Benjamite. The Israelites sent him with tribute to
Eglon king of Moab. Now Ehud had made a double-edged
sword about a foot and a half long, which he strapped to his
right thigh under his clothing. He presented the tribute to
Eglon king of Moab, who was a very fat man. After Ehud
had presented the tribute, he sent on their way the men who
had carried it. At the idols near Gilgal he himself turned
back and said, "I have a secret message for you, O king."*

*The king said, "Quiet!" And all his attendants left
him.*

*Ehud then approached him while he was sitting
alone in the upper room of his summer palace and said, "I
have a message from God for you." As the king rose from
his seat, Ehud reached with his left hand, drew the sword
from his right thigh and plunged it into the king's belly.
Even the handle sank in after the blade, which came out his
back. Ehud did not pull the sword out, and the fat closed in
over it. Then Ehud went out to the porch; he shut the doors
of the upper room behind him and locked them.*

After he had gone, the servants came and found the doors of the upper room locked. They said, "He must be relieving himself in the inner room of the house." They waited to the point of embarrassment, but when he did not open the doors of the room, they took a key and unlocked them. There they saw their lord fallen to the floor, dead.

While they waited, Ehud got away. He passed by the idols and escaped to Seirah. When he arrived there, he blew a trumpet in the hill country of Ephraim, and the Israelites went down with him from the hills, with him leading them.

"Follow me," he ordered, "for the Lord has given Moab, your enemy, into your hands." So they followed him down and, taking possession of the fords of the Jordan that led to Moab, they allowed no one to cross over. At that time they struck down about ten thousand Moabites, all vigorous and strong; not a man escaped. That day Moab was made subject to Israel, and the land had peace.

Judges 3:15-30 [NIV]

ELAM
THE
TRAVELER

3

Ah, good evening, Esteemed One. I am the inn-keeper in this caravanserai. You, I believe, are the one who will have our best room for tonight. Yes, I saw your robes, and, ah, well, they are the finest robes of all of the travelers in your particular caravan, so I just assumed... Yes, I thought so. Come in, come in! Don't wait out there with the smells of the animals and those Nabatean caravan drivers. A man of your eminence is due greater respect, and since you will be with us over the Sabbath we must get you settled into your room.

Which one? That room there by the kitchen? Oh, no! That's not yours. It's much too small for a man of your position. Your room will be that fine one up near the top of these stairs, above the sounds and smells of the camels and donkeys. That one, the one near the kitchen, already has someone in it. Who? Oh, just a man getting over being almost dead. It's a curious story, but I'm sure you... well, certainly, if you're interested, I could... very well, Esteemed One, watch your step up these stairs.

This is Friday. On the first day of this week, about, oh, it must have been about the tenth hour—the sun was almost behind the mountains—this Samaritan trader came running in with a young Jew draped across one of his donkeys. I didn't know whether to laugh at the Jew or beat the Samaritan. Then I saw blood dripping off one of the Jew's arms. Well, yes, you're correct, that would get anyone's attention!

The Jew—we later found out his name was Elam of Gadara, from up in the Decapolis—looked as if he had been fighting mountain lions. He was battered and scratched, and he was blistered from the sun. Can you believe it, he had been traveling alone—you're absolutely correct, Esteemed One, it was a stupid thing to do!—and some of our famous bandits jumped on him.

What? Elam? Just give them his money? Ooooooooh, not this one! He's strong as an ox, so he decided to fight for what he was carrying. He's barely twenty-five years old, and, naturally, he thinks he will live forever. I thought that when I was twenty-five, didn't you ?... oh, excuse me, Esteemed One, I'm sure you would never have thought such a silly... no, of course, I thought not.

At any rate, this Samaritan trader is... pardon?... Oh, I would say he's about my age, possibly a bit older, somewhere in his forties. Very serious, but rather nonde-script. You know how difficult it is to tell with those people. As I was saying, he's a regular traveler on our road. No, no, no! We never let him sleep in these rooms, particularly this one you have rented! We make him sleep out with the animals, not in here with Jews and important travelers like yourself. He said he was sitting in the shade of a palm eating when he overheard a Levite ask a priest if he had seen that dead body back along the road. Apparently the priest had seen it because he described it in great detail.

The Samaritan kept very quiet—you know how those Samaritans are, sneaky—and when the priest and Levite left, the Samaritan hurried down to the creek and found what he thought was the dead body. That was when he found that our tough little Jewish traveler wasn't quite dead! Yes, you're correct, Esteemed One, he was stupid, but he was alive. So he... who's banging on the door? Of course, foolish boy, our Esteemed Visitor wishes to wash! Just leave the water on that table.

Where was I?... the Levite, down to the creek... oh, yes. Then this Samaritan fixed up the Jew as well as he could and brought him here and put him in that room by the kitchen. You see, Elam was delirious until late Tuesday. For awhile we didn't know if he would live or die. The Samaritan never left his bedside. It was astounding. I didn't know Samaritans did things like that. Excuse me? Oh, you know, like being nice to people. Naturally, I didn't want to let the Samaritan in the room, but he paid in advance, and, of course, he was with a Jew... soooooo, I thought it was acceptable, although I'll have to have a priest or someone cleanse the room when the Jew leaves. Because the young Jew is still there! Oh, absolutely, I agree with you, the whole event was very curious.

What? Oh, yes, he's getting better. I'm taking care of him myself. Here, let me help you with those sandals, Esteemed One. All of the story? Well, it's the end of that part of the story, but the interesting part is just starting.

I was the one chosen by the Samaritan to bring the food—Elam used my dish and knife, but the Samaritan had... his name?... Hmmmm, I'm sorry, I don't think he told me... at any rate he had his own dish, and I could pour the food directly into his dish without desecrating my own pot. The Samaritan was very careful to wash properly before feeding Elam. Somewhere he learned about proper Jewish washing, and he said he didn't want to hurt Elam more than he had been hurt already. Yes, you're right, it was amazing.

Then, about sundown Tuesday, Elam came out of his stupor. I happened to be there with the evening meal when, with a gasp, Elam sat up in bed. His eyes were the size of silver pieces, but they had the color of the inside of a pig. I have never seen a worse looking man! The bandages were fresh—the Samaritan saw to that—but Elam looked like an Egyptian corpse. He blubbered and ranted and it was obvious he didn't know where he was. Then he saw the Samaritan. His scream stampeded all of the animals in the enclosure and it was all I could do to keep him from clawing the man who had saved his life.

Well, Esteemed One, it was worth the price of your whole caravan trip just to see the look on Elam's face when I told him the Samaritan saved his life. Can you believe it, I actually think for a moment he had to weigh whether it was best to be saved by a Samaritan or go ahead and die.

You remember in the scrolls the story of Jacob wrestling the angel? Well, right in that bed I watched Elam wrestle Elam. For awhile it seemed as if both would lose! The Samaritan—I wish I knew his name! I just never got around to asking—anyway, the Samaritan stood quietly in the corner until I got Elam quieted. I had to tell Elam the whole story because he couldn't remember a thing, not the trip, not the bandits, nothing. Yes, you're absolutely right, Esteemed One, a clout on the head has been known to do that; you're very perceptive and obviously well-schooled.

Elam's brain began working, but it was like watching a three-legged donkey go uphill, there was a lot of noise but not much progress. Since both hands were bandaged he couldn't feed himself. He screamed at me that no descendent of Benjamin would allow any filthy Samaritan to feed him. I had to hold him down and yell at him that the Samaritan had done what he could about ritual washings, and besides the Samaritan had fed him three or four times already.

Elam yelled at me, "Get my clothes and my donkey!"

"You don't have either," I told him. "The bandits got everything."

"Then what am I wearing?"

"The Samaritan purchased that linen saq you're wearing from me," I told him. "Otherwise, you would be naked. And as for your donkey, it's probably already been sold twice in Jerusalem." I waited a moment before telling him: "You have nothing."

"You don't understand," he snarled, "I am Elam of Gadara, and I must leave for my home in the Decapolis."

The Samaritan walked up very quiety and said, "If you move out of that bed you will break every scab and you will bleed to death before you can crawl past the caravanserai wall, because with two broken legs you most certainly cannot walk." The Samaritan—he's a tall man, very dark, with a voice like shouting in a cave—spoke as if there was no possibility of arguing with him. "When I was in Jerusalem Sunday I saw another caravan making up that was going northeast toward Gadara. It must come through here, and we can send a message to your people that way. Within a month you could get a message and possibly some money back through here. Until then, you will be in that bed. Or dead." He turned and walked out so I could reason with the hard-headed young Jew.

I tell you, Esteemed One, watching that battered face try to think was a great education for me, but not as great as the education the heart behind the battered face was receiving. Here was a Jew who had never in his life come in contact with a Samaritan—well, no, actually I haven't either, Esteemed One, and I'm quite sure you haven't... yes, I thought so—as I said, Elam had never thought of a Samaritan as someone who helps. They are, how shall I say it, a lower class of human without our sensibilities, and we Jews stay well away from them. Which is the proper thing to do, of course.

But for parts of three days, from Tuesday until yesterday noon the Samaritan did everything for Elam. He fed him—of course, not without some severe tongue-lashing by Elam about washing and protocol and those other laws of the rabbis—and he bathed him, and since Elam couldn't take care of his bodily needs, the Samaritan saw after him when he relieved himself. If it had been anyone but a Samaritan I would have thought it was beautiful, but... well, the man is a Samaritan, isn't he? And you know how they are!

Well, you must excuse me now, Esteemed One. I have to prepare your supper and... Yes, Elam is still in the small room by the kitchen. Or at least someone who looks like Elam is there. To tell you the truth, the man in the bandages doesn't look a lot like the man who came in draped across that Samaritan's donkey. His voice is different, he no longer brags about his illustrious ancestor who was a gatekeeper in King David's house of worship. Since Tuesday it seems as if his lineage isn't as important as it was when he started on this journey. And he asks instead of demanding.

And, Esteemed One, do you know the funniest thing of all? When the Samaritan left he gave me silver to pay for the young Jew's food and lodging, and he promised to pay for anything else he needed. I told that to your caravan leader, and he just laughed at me. He said it was a strange tale best kept to myself, because no one would believe me.

A man was going down from Jerusalem to Jericho, when he fell into the hands of robbers. They stripped him of his clothes, beat him and went away, leaving him half dead.

A priest happened to be going down the same road, and when he saw the man, he passed by on the other side. So too, a Levite, when he came to the place and saw him, passed by on the other side.

But a Samaritan, as he traveled, came where the man was; and when he saw him, he took pity on him. He went to him and bandaged his wounds, pouring on oil and wine. Then he put the man on his own donkey, took him to an inn and took care of him. The next day he took out two silver coins and gave them to the innkeeper. "Look after him," he said, "and when I return, I will reimburse you for any extra expense you may have."

Which of these three do you think was a neighbor to the man who fell into the hands of robbers?

Luke 10:30-36 [NIV]

THE JAILKEEPER

4

Damon the jailkeeper was obviously angry. Actually, he was frightened, but for the squat, thick-shouldered man fright always took the public face of anger. His bulging thighs and veined calves strained at the leather thongs criss-crossing them as he angled quickly up the dark cobble-stoned street toward his simple home. He slowed as that nagging conversation with those two Jews from Palestine grabbed at his mind. But greater than the Jews was the memory of the last meeting with the priestesses and the final meeting with them scheduled for tonight. He twisted through the low rock wall surrounding their small house. "Lymnia? Wife!"

She hurried through the door, some sewing still in her hands. "Why were you running?" she asked nervously. "Did a prisoner escape?"

He waved her into silence. "You know better. If that happened I would be down in the jail myself, dead on my sword. Those are the rules." He paced the tiny front room of the three room house like a caged animal. "I had to talk to you. Do you remember those two Jews I told you about?"

"The ones from Palestine?"

"Yes, those two." He slumped onto a handmade stool, rough and solid like its owner. "I just put them in jail for something they probably didn't do... but that's common enough. Yesterday, I heard one of the Jews speak in the marketplace, and I thought they might cause trouble, so I followed them."

Lymnia frowned uncertainly. "You didn't tell me that."

"I... didn't want to concern you with my work." Both of them knew that was a transparent lie. For many months he had been telling her everything about everything. She became his guidepost in his quest for information, the chart keeping him from blind-ended questioning. "I was told they were down near the river, so I went there. One of them began talking... to a woman."

"A Jew? Talking to a woman where people could watch?" Suddenly her interest fired. "About what?"

"His religion."

"About his gods?" She couldn't believe it. "A Jew talking to a woman?" She drew back, wary at this line of talk. Her husband's broad face was fixed and unsmiling, not that a smile would improve the craggy visage that much. Although the lineage of the ancient Greeks forged his mind, his barbarian blood diluted the classic features into a thick-

nosed, scowling countenance. That, and his unpopular job, made him and his family virtually outcasts in this riverside city of the Roman province of Macedonia.

Of course, that was only the exterior man, the part the Captain of the Roman garrison saw. And valued. Damon the jailkeeper was that rarity among Roman hirelings, an honest man. He lived on his salary, he took no bribes... and he was illiterate, with all that went with that word. Lymnia knew of his burning fight to learn, but there was no precedent for a man, a worker, learning to read. He came from a rural area north of Macedonia where learning was not only frowned on, it was actually feared. Nevertheless, the hunger for knowledge remained, particularly knowledge of the gods.

And now, with age, that craving was expanding. He spent more and more time on solitary walks peering out toward the sea or upward toward the high ridge behind his town, forcing his mind through the labyrinths of the ancient

Greek philosophies, those few scattered ideas he picked up from chance encounters with rich men or wandering scholars. He always came home from his trudging, muttering walks with some fumbling inquiries for Lymnia which seemed to bubble up from some passionate caldron of ignorance.

She glanced at the stolid face twisted with what she first thought was concentration, but which she now knew to be fear.

"Damon." She waited apprehensively until he brought his tumbling thoughts back under control. "Don't talk about the Jews now. Will we be walking to the meeting of the Melissae when the moon rises tonight?" A plain woman, worn from low pay and social nonacceptance, she brushed a stray wisp of hair with a nervous gesture. Her thin, bony face searched his broad, flat one for signs of understanding. She knew Damon feared the blue-robed priestesses as she also feared them, but for the sake of the future of her daughter, and for her own standing in the community, the fear had to be conquered.

Damon rubbed his rough hands nervously on his skirt-robe. He remembered taking Lymnia to such a meeting. Never had Damon experienced such a fiery passion in his soul. He, with his history of total control of his mind and actions, found he could not stop his body from twitching at the constantly repeated rhythms of the two sweating drummers and the nasal whine of the reedy aulos. The wailing chant-like music and the flickering lanterns virtually robbed them of their minds while they sat cowering in the old quarry. He feared the Melissae, those priestesses of the Earth Mother, as he feared no other person or thing.

"That's why we must talk," Damon said rapidly. "I heard fantastic words from those two Jews. They talked to this cloth seller, and then..."

"Are we going to the meeting of the Melissae tonight?" Her voice strained at the words.

"That's why I have to talk to you. These Jews... "

"NO!" she interrupted angrily. "The priestesses have demanded our decision tonight." She turned nervously. "You know how important it is... for our daughter."

The jailkeeper struggled to control his agitation. He pulled in a deep breath, then let it escape slowly. "Yes," he said carefully. "I know how she will be accepted in this town... and so will we as never before if we allow our daughter to do what those other priestesses do." Suddenly, his fragile control shattered. He leaped up, his fists clenched. Lymnia cowered as if he were about to strike her. "Those women, with their incense and strange music, they invite special men, the rich ones, into their little 'worship' rooms and they... "

"NO! They are our priestesses! They are our own voices to our gods." Lymnia clamped her hands over her ears. "They have chosen our daughter. They choose only one each season, and this is for the Spring, the most important time of the year. With our daughter's beauty she will soon be one of the leaders, and you know what that means for us." She leaned closer, her eyes brimming with tears. "We will be accepted by our neighbors. The entire city will know us. We will be more than..."

" ...than just a jailer and his wife?" He shrugged, but he still had to say what touched him so deeply less than an hour before. "Wife, we will attend the Melissae gathering when the moon rises, but first you must hear me. Sit." She dropped onto a piece of worn carpet as he paced the tiny room.

"You remember what it was like, that visit to the Melissae? There was darkness and that strange smell of incense. You remember how we tried to whisper, but something, the incense, or what they gave us to drink, or something, blinded our minds." Damon stood transfixed as the fear returned. "Do you remember when we tried to talk all we had were simple words, like children." His voice became a hoarse whisper. "They stole our minds that night, Lymnia... as they will steal our daughter's mind for her entire life."

The hands of the frail, desperate woman clenched into pale claws as remembrance flowed through a reluctant mind. "But this is the way of our people, Damon," she sobbed. "These are our priestesses who speak for our gods. The Melissae come from here, in Philippi." Her voice trailed off into a keening moan. "And... they need our daughter, for our city."

The jailer fell to his knees before his shattered wife. "Lymnia... Wife... listen to this question. I have bored and tortured you with my questions for months and years." He lifted her tear-stained and frightened face. His voice spoke with an unaccustomed gentleness. "But you must listen to one more question, and this time it must be you who speaks."

She looked up, startled at the remarkable change in this voice she remembered but had not heard for so many years. She nodded dully.

"I followed the two Jews and watched as they talked to the seller of bright cloth about this great single god of theirs, and how the god had a son who was the true ruler of the earth. But... "—Damon's voice broke at the remembrance—"both the father-god and the son-god ruled with kindness, and love... and each man and woman—do you hear me, Wife?—each man and each woman must be thought of as a child of that father-god and a sister to that son-god. Then the father-god will take care of each of his children as a father down here takes care of and loves his own child." He dropped to the floor before her. "Now, you must answer this question." Gently, as if cradling a fragile flower, Damon cupped Lymnia's face in his hands. "Do the Melissae love your daughter as you love her, and for the same reason?"

Lymnia threw back her head as if to take a breath, but only a rasping wail came out. All the years of frustration and social ostracism boiled to the surface. She knew what the Melissae could do for her... but at the cost of her daughter. She felt her husband's lips touch her forehead. Then he held her and rocked her, lightly, like a sick child. He had never touched her this way, not in their entire lives.

The tenderness in his voice was like a gentle breeze. "This question is the one you must answer, Wife. Our daughter is the die which will be thrown." He glanced through the small, crude window. "The moon has risen. In a few minutes we must go. Sleep a while, and then answer the question."

He pulled Lymnia's head over on his shoulder as he lay on the rough texture of the rug. A great wave of relief, like cool water on a fevered face, fell over Damon. He had said it! He actually put his thoughts and his words together without muttering or stammering, and he even used some of the words of those two Jews. Like a sea mist blowing away, his mind cleared. Unaccountably, he slept.

Suddenly, some dust dropped from the ceiling of their small room onto his face, then the timbers framing the small house groaned. Groggily, Damon leaped to his feet. He shouted as he yanked Lymnia through the door. "Earthquake! Get outside. We must... the jail! If the earthquake hits the jail the prisoners... " He lost the rest of the sentence in a grunt as he climbed on top of the earthen fence. In the flickering glare Damon saw a huge billowing dust cloud wreathe the jail itself. Horror-stricken, he climbed down and grabbed his wife in a fierce embrace. "I must go to the jail."

"NO!" She stumbled as she reached for him, trying with her slight body to block his path to almost sure death. "You can't go. If a prisoner has escaped... " Her tightening throat cut off the rest of the sentence.

"Wife," Damon said roughly, "I have lived my life with honesty, and I will keep it with me for as long as it is possible." He started to run, but stopped abruptly and turned. She stood transfixed by his level stare. "Lymnia, hear me well. If I do not return, you know that you will have to make the decision about the Melissae. Think of the gods... all of them." Then he broke into a stomping run through the rough, dark streets toward the jail.

About midnight Paul and Silas were praying and singing hymns to God, and the other prisoners were listening to them. Suddenly there was such a violent earthquake that the foundations of the prison were shaken. At once all the prison doors flew open, and everybody's chains came loose. The jailer woke up, and when he saw the prison doors open, he drew his sword and was about to kill himself because he thought the prisoners had escaped. But Paul shouted, "Don't harm yourself! We are all here!"

The jailer called for lights, rushed in and fell trembling before Paul and Silas. He then brought them out and asked, "Men, what must I do to be saved?"

They replied, "Believe in the Lord Jesus, and you will be saved—you and your household." Then they spoke the word of the Lord to him and to all the others in his house. At that hour of the night the jailer took them and washed their wounds; then immediately he and all his family were baptized. The jailer brought them into his house and set a meal before them, and the whole family was filled with joy, because they had come to believe in God.

Acts 16:25-34 [NIV]

THE OFFICIAL FROM THE UPPER NILE

5

The four matched gray horses stood quietly, the trace lines to the richly painted and carved chariot drooping into the hot Jerusalem dust. Suddenly Tobiah turned from the Roman tax official and the Jewish banker he was talking with. He snapped his fingers at the soldier loading one of the packhorses. "Fix the loose strap," he said firmly. Immediately two other soldiers ran to help the first one tug at a leather belt holding several large bundles on the horse's wooden pack-frame. Then Tobiah turned back to the two men standing subserviantly in the Judean heat.

"Excuse me for that interruption. Those bundles of Parthian silks are for her royal highness, the Queen. Now, about those ships... " Tobiah spoke in short, accurate sentences. He never wasted words. He knew his own time was valuable, and he assumed the same for others. To the dark, intense man a word saved was a second saved, a trait which procured and kept his job as royal treasurer.

"Oh, yes, the ships from Thrace!" The thin, bent Jewish banker-official nodded appreciatively as he touched the cool embroidered seat on the chariot. "I can guarantee two trips each year from Caesarea to Alexandria and from there up the Nile to your city." Absently, the banker rubbed the fine carvings on the four-wheeled vehicle's gate-door.

"Thank you, honorable Zillethai." Tobiah bowed slightly, his loose linen traveling robe swirling in the morning breeze. "My Queen will be pleased with the increased trade with Judea and Rome. I have written a letter to your ambassador commending your work." The Jewish official smiled broadly and started to speak, but Tobiah held up his hand. "And you, Hermonaeus, have been equally helpful with your work in the customs house. The Roman commander has been notified of your good work. I have left small gifts—from my Queen, of course—at each of your homes. Now," he lowered his voice as he turned away from the soldiers packing the horses, "I have one last request, and it is very important. Please tell me about this carpenter-rabbi I hear mentioned in the streets."

Hermonaeus, the stocky Roman customs officer, drew back, his eyes squinting slightly. Before he could speak, Zillethai, the Jewish banker, bustled in with his nervous, excited voice. "He was the leader of this new sect. I believe they call themselves Christians, and I'll tell you they cause us Jews an extreme amount of trouble. As a Jew, you should best forget them and their obscure leader. They also give the Romans too much trouble." He nodded deferentially toward the Roman official. Then he hesitated. "Where, may I ask, did you hear of this heretic carpenter?"

"It doesn't matter. I heard. And what I hear is interesting." He turned at a curse from one of the soldier-guards traveling with him. "I'm leaving within the hour, and I wanted to know more." He sighed wearily. "I read many scrolls, but nothing seems to make sense. I need a teacher or rabbi like this carpenter to carry back to the Upper Nile region. I am one of a handful of Jews in our capitol city, and I'm the only one who can read the scrolls. I need much help with my Hebrew. "

Zillethai's eyes widened. "I noticed the scroll in the seat of your fine chariot, but I assumed it would be for.. that is, I didn't realize ..."

"That I read Hebrew? Each year I travel down the Nile to Alexandria on the Queen's business, and each trip I study with a rabbi there. Unfortunately, I can read more than I can understand. My desire reaches farther than the light from my lamp." He sighed quietly. "Possibly later a rabbi will..." He left the sentence hanging as he clapped his

hands. Immediately the ten soldier-guards mounted their horses. The chariot driver and Tobiah's personal servant scrambled quickly onto the seat of the chariot. Tobiah grasped the handled of the chariot's gate-door. "The sun does not wait. I must go. Thank you, Zillethai, for your help. It will be remembered. Now, I need some instructions for my journey from Hermonaeus, so..."

Zillethai's eyes narrowed into slits. "Yes, yes, of course! Absolutely, I understand." He bowed carefully, like a thin waterbird, then began backing away. "May your journey be swift and safe, and may Jehovah protect you." He turned and walking away slowly, his suspicious gaze flickering back to the Roman tax gatherer and the rich foreign official.

Tobiah waited until Zillethai was out of earshot, then began pointing toward the Jerusalem gate leading toward the Gaza road. "Hermonaeus, we will speak your Roman language, since my soldiers do not understand it. I will wave and point toward the road, and you do the same. But we will speak of this carpenter." Although his hand aimed out the gate, his eyes searched the broad face of the Roman. "When I mentioned him a few minutes ago, your voice said nothing, but your face told me you knew something of him. Tell me... please."

Hermonaeus waited long moments before answering. Finally, he said, "As a soldier of Rome I'm supposed to stay far away from the local religions. However"— he looked up at Tobiah's intense face—"as I understand it, the carpenter was a kind of traveling teacher, a wise man who roamed these hills." The Roman official swept his hand in a small arc as if describing a pass through the Judean hills. "He's dead now. Crucified, I believe."

"Crucified!" The intensity of Tobiah's voice startled the Roman official. "Hermonaeus, now both your eyes and voice betray you. You know more than this. Please, I must know whatever you can tell me about this carpenter-rabbi."

Hermonaeus bent as if drawing a map in the dirt. "Now, my friend, it is your eyes and voice that betray you. Why such a great strength? You have been in Jerusalem only, what, three weeks? You have concluded many business dealings for your Queen. You have lived in a rented palace, your clothes are sewn with gold thread, each meal you eat is rich and varied, your chariot is known throughout the city for its splendor." He looked up, his gaze searching the treasurer's face. "I believe I glimpse something behind your words, as the carpenter saw behind my own."

Tobiah dropped to his knees. "You knew him?"

"No. I only heard him. Once, from far back in the crowd. But it was enough. Such things you never forget."

"Could he answer questions?" Tobiah grabbed the Roman's plain linen cloak "Was he as wise as people say?"

"Wiser."

Tobias bent closer, his voice tight. "Wiser? How so?"

"He used plain words to explain the so-called wisdom of the rabbis. No one could best him at teaching. And his teachings meant the same to Jews or Romans or Egyptians. His words had no limits. Old or young, educated or plain, everyone, I'm telling you everyone understood him." Suddenly Hermonaeus shrugged elaborately. He had spoken too much. "But you would not be interested in his speeches. You already have everything."

Tobiah buried his head in his hands. For most of a minute he struggled to swallow the fist-sized knot in his throat. Everything? When he lowered his hands he wiped away long rivulets of tears. "Ah, my Roman friend, your eyes see some things, but not the terror in the heart beating under these expensive robes. For half of my life I have served my Queen, and as you say, I have been paid well. But a reason for existence does not come from a hoard of gold coins. I have looked for wisdom, but it is not in the power given me by my Queen. The power of my office is like a fistful of water. The body you see is clothed well, but the spirit is dying."

"Dying? In that royal chariot worth five years of my wages?"

"My Queen insists that I travel in a manner to bring her glory. But when I stop by a stream and I take off these rich robes to bathe, I know that this naked body must be worth more than the robes that hang on a bramble. Where does the worth of a man come from? Sitting in a golden chariot? Eating rich food from silver bowls? Snapping your fingers at guards?"

"The carpenter could have told you," Hermonaeus said simply.

"Yes, everywhere I hear about his wisdom, his art of explaining. But he's dead now. Crucified, you believe." The words echoed like a whip's snap. "And I am left to go back to a distant town and struggle through the scrolls of our law by myself. Don't you understand that I cannot teach others what I do not know myself! This is the first time I have been to Jerusalem. All my life I have lived for this moment... and I go away empty! I am like a jar that someone paints and then places far back in a cave where no one can fill it. I have money and I have power, and still I have nothing! The few words of that carpenter that I have heard have been like great treasures, but there are so many more questions I must have answered. I have scrolls of almost all of the sacred writings, but they make little sense. I bought this scroll of the prophet Isaiah's writings, and I will read it on my journey home. I am a Jew in a distant land. I am rich, I am powerful . . . and I am alone." His head dropped so the soldiers could not see the tears rolling down his face. "I am alone because I am ignorant of what my God wants from me. I have no way of knowing the reason my God has kept me alive."

Hermonaeus touched Tobiah's sleeve. "Your soldiers are confused. Do you want to stay awhile at my house?"

"No!" Tobiah struggled to his feet, his head once again erect and proud. "I will read the scrolls again, although ignorance repeated is still ignorance. Thank you, friend Hermonaeus. I will send a message when I get to my city on the Upper Nile." He climbed slowly into his chariot as he gazed at Jerusalem with sad eyes. "I came here needing so much. I'm taking away so little."

"If I hear of any good words of wisdom I will send them on to you by your messengers."

Tobiah clapped his hands and the lead soldier turned. "Take us down the Gaza road." As the chariot creaked forward he turned to Hermonaeus. "By the way, what was the carpenter's name?"

"It was a common name. Nothing special. Jesus, I believe it was."

Now an angel of the Lord said to Philip, "Go south to the road—the desert road—that goes down from Jerusalem to Gaza." So he started out, and on his way he met an Ethiopian eunuch, an important official in charge of all the treasury of Candace, queen of the Ethiopians. This man had gone to Jerusalem to worship, and on his way home was sitting in his chariot reading the book of Isaiah the prophet. The Spirit told Philip, "Go to that chariot and stay near it."

Then Philip ran up to the chariot and heard the man reading Isaiah the prophet. "Do you understand what you are reading?" Philip asked.

"How can I," he said, "unless someone explains it to me?" So he invited Philip to come up and sit with him.

The eunuch was reading this passage of Scripture:

"He was led like a sheep to the slaughter,

and as a lamb before the shearer is silent,

so he did not open his mouth.

In his humiliation he was deprived of justice.

Who can speak of his descendants?

For his life was taken from the earth."

The eunuch asked Philip, "Tell me, please, who is the prophet talking about, himself or someone else?" Then Philip began with that very passage of Scripture and told him the good news about Jesus.

As they traveled along the road, they came to some water and the eunuch said, "Look, here is water. Why shouldn't I be baptized?" And he ordered the chariot to stop. Then both Philip and the eunuch went down into the water and Philip baptized him. When they came up out of the water, the Spirit of the Lord suddenly took Philip away, and the eunuch did not see him again, but went on his way rejoicing.

Acts 8:26-39 [NIV]

THE
ROYAL
OFFICIAL'S
DYING SON

6

Journal entry: Sunday

Cyprian is still sick. The fever makes his eyes red,
and they have begun gazing around the room instead of
focusing on his mother or me. He is slow answering when
we call his name. I have been to every physician and
prayed to every god in the Roman listing; what else can I
do?

Herod Antipas, Tetrarch of Galilee, by the hand of his private secretary

To Palatinus, trusted Royal Official in Capernaum:

Greetings!

I write that you may know about my concern with this new itinerant Jewish holy man. Quite a number of people are following him, or at least honoring him. I have heard strange and conflicting stories about them.

I write asking you to send me a report concerning their actions; are they dangerous, is their holy man dangerous, what does he want from me, that sort of thing. My royal brother, Archelaus, is having trouble with another group of Jews in Judea and Samaria, and I wish to avoid controversy as much as possible.

My secretary informs me your son is ill. Accept my royal concern. I will give an offering to the priestess on his behalf.

Hurry your report.

Palatinus, Palace Official assigned to Capernaum

To His Royal Majesty, Herod Antipas, Tetrarch of Galilee, Son of Herod the Great, and Brother to other Great Rulers, Near and Far

Greetings:

I am constantly thankful to our Roman gods for your good health, most excellent Antipas. May you live long and rule well as you have always done.

In answer to your letter, I have sent messages to those serving under me requesting information concerning this Galilean who is preaching in your area. I will add them to my own investigations and send a full report within this week.

Also, I thank you sincerely for your interest in my son's health. Unfortunately, he continues to waste away. We have consulted the best Roman physicians, but they have no explanation about his fever, which seems to almost burn away his flesh. But excuse my personal problems, which are as nothing compared to the weight of your royal responsibilities. I thank you for the offering to the priestesses. Possibly these things take more time than I wish to endure.

That minor official from Seleucia just returned for his annual business trip up north. He heard this carpenter-teacher speak. The official says this teacher, whose name is Jesus, heals leprosy and blindness. When I told him no one could heal leprosy or blindness, he just smiled and said, "I was there."

Palatinus, in the Royal Residence in Capernaum

To my esteemed friend Sextus in Capitolinas of the Decapolis

My sincerest greetings and respect for our continued friendship:

You must know our years and decades of friendship are a great treasure in my life, particularly now that anguish over my son's mysterious illness takes so much of my daily effort and attention.

His Royal Majesty Herod Antipas has requested information concerning this group which follows some Jewish carpenter-rabbi. I understand they are some sort of Jewish splinter group. His Royal Majesty wishes to know more of the inner workings of their beliefs, if there is any danger, what they think of Roman rule, and anything else you deem important for my report. Also, do they have any particular and unique abilities, either militarily or with witchcraft?

Now for a final personal request, and please understand my fear at being so bold: do you know of any knowledge or ability which those Jews or that itinerant rabbi might have which would benefit my son? Sextus, I have heard strange things about this wandering teacher. I realize the danger from asking such a question, but it is nothing compared to the danger my son is in. He was such a fine, strong boy, bright-eyed and with a good mind, and now his fever has caused him to waste away to bones and skin. And my wife's mental condition has deteriorated with my son's health. You must realize how desperate I am if I even consider consulting a non-Roman about my son's illness. I treasure your judgment in such things, and I wait for your answer.

Sextus, a Royal Scribe in service to his Majesty in Capitolinus

To Palatinus, my treasured friend of my boyhood

This note is scribbled in haste to catch the Royal Messenger who leaves within the hour.

I made discrete inquiry, and this person's name is Jesus, although some are calling him Messiah, which is some sort of deliverer. He claims to perform miracles, and (I hesitate to tell you this) there is even a rumor he brought a child, a widow's son I believe it was, back to life. From the reports I have heard this roving teacher is not attempting to gain a following, but that message seems to have the opposite effect: hundreds are going out in the countryside to hear him. However, I hear of no rebellions being promoted.

I have one final question: Palatinus, has the Galilean sun baked your brain? In one breath you ask about this wandering Jew, and in the next you wonder if you should go to him for help! I would have thought you would be too well educated to believe in such people (your word "witchcraft" was well chosen). As a friend I'm trying to evaluate your position in the service of His Royal Majesty. You must be very circumspect. Are there no decent Roman physicians in all of Capernaum or Galilee? They would be much safer, as well as better educated.

The Royal Messenger's horse just arrived, so I must close. Palatinus, honor our friendship and stay far away from this Jewish teacher. He was a carpenter, if you can believe it, before he took up preaching! Your career is a fine one, and I would rather visit you in the Capernaum palace than in the Capernaum jail!

Where can I take Cyprian that I have not already taken him? Of whom shall I inquire about his fever? I sit in my house and look at him, and I know I have no power to help. He was always large for his age, but now he has wasted until his eyes are hollow and his skin sags on his body. The demon in him is trying to kill him, and Cyprian is too young to understand. I sing him little songs, and I wonder about my own mind. Will I ever understand why a child must endure such sickness?

A servant mentioned this Jesus who is supposed to have great powers of healing. But he's up in the hill country near Cana, and a Jew would never travel this far to help a Roman!

To the Honorable Palatinus, Royal Servant to His Majesty Herod Antipas:

As a high priestess in the Temple of the Earth Mother it has come to my attention that your son is gravely ill. I have often had opportunity to see such sickness before. I believe this illness is due to your lack of interest in the offerings to our Temple. If you would take advantage of the Women of the Mysteries, and, of course, make an offering appropriate to your high station in His Majesty's service, I can guarantee a full recovery by your son.

Cyprian is sicker than yesterday. I have just been to the Physician again, but he seems as mystified by the illness as we are. The boy's fever has gone even higher, if my touch can be trusted. I pray to our gods that at least my touch will remain, since I fear for my mind. The anguish over my son's illness had taken most of my waking hours, and even at night I cannot sleep for waiting for his coming death.

Always on my mind: what can I do that has not already been done? Have I left some prayer unsaid, some offering unassigned? The priestesses of the Mystery Temple have asked for donations, so my wife has taken them most of my salary. She believes in the priestesses, but I do not. I have never seen any proof of their ability. But if it helps my wife...

A servant of my wife mentioned Jesus, the wandering Jewish teacher from Nazareth. From what she says he has done some startling things. If I could leave my son for a day I would travel to Cana and see if I could hire this preacher to come and try to heal Cyprian. Who knows? Possibly he knows some magic, some incantation which would help.

From Napolitus the Physician

To Palatinus, Servant to King Antipas the Tetrarch

Do this, and the boy may live:

Spread his body with the finest olive oil twice a day.

Have him bled, but quickly before the evil in his blood kills him.

Take him to the mineral baths the other side of the Salt Sea, although his condition may preclude the last named.

Prepare your mind; he is very weak.

Journal entry: Tuesday

My son is too weak to raise his head. The light blue of his eyes, which reminds his mother of that lake near her home in Cappadocia, has faded to the color of mist. It has been twelve weeks since he fell ill, but it seems like twelve years. To watch a small boy fight what he does not understand is both frightening and saddening. I have run out of words for explaining his sickness to him.

Should I go to the Canaanite shrine where my wife is praying? Should I give greater gifts to the priestesses of the Earth Mother? Should I risk taking my son on an overland journey to the salt baths when the trip itself might kill him?

I overheard a soldier talking, and it seems this carpenter/teacher Jesus is staying in Cana and doing some unbelievable things there. If I could only believe that what I hear is true. If he could cure Cyprian I would pay him everything I have. If he requires my worship... I would do that also. I have never seen another man worthy of worship, but perhaps this one could be.

To my wife:

Cyprian no longer recognizes me. The physician says my son will die tonight.

I have personally questioned seven people who have talked with this Jesus, and I have read several letters from other officials, and the witnesses are too great to discount. These are not ignorant beggars; they are intelligent merchants and government officials. They stand quietly as they list the good the man does, the miracles and the healings and the wise sayings.

My wife, I must go to find this Jesus. Since my sanity and my reason for living will die with Cyprian I have nothing to lose by searching out this carpenter-teacher. When you return from the Temple of the Mysteries I will be gone.

From an early history of the carpenter-teacher:

Once more he visited Cana in Galilee, where he had turned the water into wine. And there was a certain royal official whose son lay sick at Capernaum. When this man heard that Jesus had arrived in Galilee from Judea, he went to him and begged him to come and heal his son, who was close to death.

"Unless you people see miraculous signs and wonders," Jesus told him, "you will never believe."

The royal official said, "Sir, come down before my child dies."

Jesus replied, "You may go. Your son will live."

The man took Jesus at his word and departed. While he was still on the way, his servants met him with the news that his boy was living. When he inquired as to the time when his son had gotten better, they said to him, "The fever left him yesterday at the seventh hour."

Then the father realized that this was the exact time at which Jesus had said to him, "Your son will live." So he and all his household believed.

John 4:46-53 [NIV]

THE FINAL GIFT

7

Old Barzillai tossed the last thick sheaf of wheat on the stack next to his cow stalls, then sagged against the high mud and stone fence surrounding his barns. The weariness that washed over him was like a warm wave on the Salt Sea. It has been years—no, it seemed like decades—since he had been this tired ... or this exhilarated. His flushed and lined face glistened in the dimming light of evening. He turned at a footstep behind him. His son hesitated, then came closer.

"Did you finish feeding the cattle, Kimham?"

"Yes," the broad-shouldered young man said simply. Kimham, almost twenty-five years old and strong as an ox, stooped to straighten some stones on the fence. It was obvious something was bothering Barzillai's only son.

Even with his dim vision, Old Barzillai could see the young man's strength and vitality. He could also hear the barely disguised anger.

"Father." The urgency in the single word turned Barzillai's head. "I heard, I mean, there is a rumor that the king wants you to live in his palace." He hesitated, then said, "Have you heard anything about that?"

Barzillai nodded slowly. "I have heard such talk."

Kimham waited, then his impatience boiled over. "Well? What will you tell the king? Will you go with him?"

Barzillai looked out over the wide expanse of his fields. Sheep grazed placidly on a patch of green around his best spring. "What do you think? If you were answering, what would you say to the king?"

"I would say... you have worked hard your entire life. Look at the size of your grain bins. You have more shepherds than most people have sheep. These lands have made you rich, but it's because you have worked harder than anyone here. You've earned your last years in the king's palace."

"And if I wish to stay on my farm? As you said, I've worked my entire life for these lands and herds."

The stocky young man could not stand still. He frowned, then grabbed a flat stone and hammered at a stake holding the gate. "It's time for you to rest."

"And what about the people of this village? As one of the elders I listen to many people. I hear their problems, and with my riches I help them."

"As I said, you've earned your time of quiet." Kimham's voice was flat and strained. He bunched his shoulders, a nervous habit Barzillai had noticed the past few months. "Father, what will you say to the king?"

Barzillai peered out over his large estate. He squinted against the sun in a useless attempt to get past the cloudiness which had come over his eyes within the past year. "Kimham, I'm eighty years old, and for the first time in a score of years I am looking forward to tomorrow... and to tomorrow's tomorrow."

Kimham snorted as he threw down the stone he had used for pounding. "All of this began when you fed David's men, didn't it?"

"Of course! For years nothing interested me. I was just another old man waiting to die. Then, suddenly one of my shepherds ran up with the news that the king was nearby and needed help." Barzillai straightened, the old fire blazing in his eyes. "Well, when I heard that God's anointed was near, I sent messages to my friends Shobi and Makir, and we strapped on our armor and called out our fighting men. Then we gathered provisions for... "

"Yes, I already know all of that. If you'll remember, you made me ride one of the carts." The stocky, intense young man clenched and released his fists. "I asked you if you were going to go talk with the king?"

Without thinking, Barzillai flexed his own rough hands. The sheaves of straw he had been stacking glistened gold in the fading sunlight. Although the colors were distinct, he was having more and more trouble discerning the texture of the wheat, just as he could not smell the sweetness of the new-cut grain as clearly as when he was younger.

"And you, Kimham... what would you do if I went to the palace?"

The young man's eyes widened at the question. "I suppose I could stay here, on the farm, with my wife and son. If I stayed here I would take charge of the herd of goats and enlarge the cheese house. The barley fields need to be expanded, and I just heard that the farm to the east is for sale." A curious excitement, like a distant flash of lightning, charged his words. "I also know that I—we—could borrow some money to build an inn on the road to Jerusalem, and I would take my family and... "

Old Barzillai stood peering at this son of his old age, unable to believe what he was hearing. Kimham leave these lands? It was unthinkable that his son would want to leave what had been built for him. A father builds to give away, not to keep. All of these lands and flocks were for Kimham. Couldn't he understand that? You can't walk away from a gift that took a lifetime to build.

"Kimham, think about this next question care-fully." The young man bent forward. "If I died tonight, what would you do next month?"

"Father, you're not going to... are you feeling ill, is that why you asked me that?"

"I have not felt this good in years. But I need to know what you are thinking."

"My true thoughts?" Kimham asked slowly. He turned to look at the barns and animal pens. Then his gaze swung out past the village of Rogelim to the hills and the Jerusalem road beyond. "My true thoughts are... that I should build another house and an inn on the road beyond our farm to the west. There are many more travelers now than when I was a child, and a caravansarie would be very profitable. Then, we could sell our milk and cheese and barley bread to travelers who pay high prices for good food and a safe bed. And I could establish a store house and an inn up in Jerusalem for our cheeses and breads. We make the best now, and we could make more with ease." Kimham's words and thoughts tumbled over each other. His face flushed with the pure joy of building idea on idea. Suddenly he stopped. "But, of course, you will stay with your farm. I can hear it in your voice."

"My farm? It's your farm, too."

"Never! You own it and you run it. You always have, you always will." The young man threw up his hands, then turned abruptly and strode off. He glanced back briefly to say, "You will be here forever! And so will I, because I have nothing of my own. Everything is yours."

The old man wanted to speak, to call after the stocky, headstrong young man and tell him that everything was his, but a sudden memory bound Barzillai as if with leather thongs. It was more than his son's words; it was the reverberant sound of resentment and frustration spilling out. Barzillai recognized the sound far too well. Life was calling to Kimham, but he couldn't answer. Just as life called to Barzillai long years before.

Like an echo long forgotten, Barzillai heard his own words ringing from over half a century in the past. He had worked for his father until he had a wife and four children, and over and over his father promised Barzillai would own the family's holdings near Kir-Moab. But his father seemed to get stronger, not weaker with the years. Although Barzillai had been a man with a family, his father treated him as a small boy. Always he answered to his father. He made no decisions for himself. Nothing was his own, neither the triumphs nor the mistakes. And certainly none of the land or flocks were his. He might as well have been a pauper; he could call nothing his own. He remembered his anger building like a thunderhead with a strident bitterness that at times threatened to destroy both himself and his family. His wrath grew as he waited, and waited... and waited.

Barzillai looked toward his village of Rogelim, dimly visible in the distance. These were his people, the field workers and shepherds who worked for him, and much of his grain and cheese went to feed them and the people of Rogelim. He knew every rock on these hills and plains as clearly as he knew the cracks in the scrolls he kept displayed in his house. Maybe clearer, he thought, now that my eyes have begun to cloud.

"Then that's it!," he said suddenly. "Succeeding is meaningless when someone else makes the decision. My son wants his own chance to fail, just as I had my own chance. And a father's final decision is... " He nodded without speaking further. He had his answer.

He walked rapidly toward his large house. "Kimham! Kimham! Come, we must be going." His son stood tying a cow to a fence. "The king must not be kept waiting."

"Then you're going?"

"My son, an iron blade will wear away or it will rust away." He smiled at his son's frown. "I prefer the first. But now, we must talk to the king."

Barzillai the Gileadite also came down from Rogelim to cross the Jordan with the king and to send him on his way from there. Now Barzillai was a very old man, eighty years of age. He had provided for the king during his stay in Mahanaim, for he was a very wealthy man. The king said to Barzillai, "Cross over with me and stay with me in Jerusalem, and I will provide for you."

But Barzillai answered the king, "How many more years will I live, that I should go up to Jerusalem with the king? I am now eighty years old. Can I tell the difference between what is good and what is not? Can your servant taste what he eats and drinks? Can I still hear the voices of men and women singers? Why should your servant be an added burden to my lord the king? Your servant will cross over the Jordan with the king for a short distance, but why should the king reward me in this way? Let your servant return, that I may die in my own town near the tomb of my father and mother. But here is your servant Kimham. Let him cross over with my lord the king. Do for him whatever pleases you."

The king said, "Kimham shall cross over with me, and I will do for him whatever pleases you. And anything you desire for me I will do for you."

So all the people crossed the Jordan, and then the king crossed over. The king kissed Barzillai and gave him his blessing, and Barzillai returned to his home.

II Sam. 19:31-39 [NIV]

MATTHIAS, THE NOBODY

8

Little Donkey, if you did not listen so well, I would have grilled you for supper long ago! And don't twist your ear like that, you know what I'm saying. Just keep walking, although you might move a bit faster. It's not as if I sent that message. Peter sent it! If that doesn't impress you, it certainly impresses me.

Oh, yes, now your other ear twists around. Let me say it louder: Peter sent the message! I don't doubt that you're asking yourself, "Why Matthias!? Why should that plain man, that nobody who rides me get a note from the great Christian Peter?"

Certainly you should—Watch out for that ledge!—yes, certainly you should ask that. The man who rides you is a nobody. If I add up the letters of my name it is no number at all. "Matthias? Who is that?," everyone says. And they are right to say it.

You remember, don't you, Donkey, when the Master sent us out with all of those other fine men, Justus and the rest? Yes, bob your head. You remember. We were to go ahead of him into those towns he listed, and we were to do all those great things, those spectacular works that... What? Why are you twisting your head, Donkey? No, I... I truly can not call them... miracles. They were great works, but they were not... miracles. Matthias the Nobody cannot perform miracles. The Twelve, they can perform MIRACLES, but as you know—as everyone knows—I'm nothing compared to them.

Why are you walking so slowly? Oh, the sun. Yes, I see it's high enough for a rest. And, of course, you saw me tie a water skin on my belt. Very well, half for you and half for me, but watch out for robbers. In addition to being a nobody, your owner is not very bright. We should have waited until tomorrow's caravan formed for the trip to Jerusalem. You see, don't you, that if I could perform miracles I would lift us up and place us gently in the street where Peter and the rest of the great believers meet. Then I wouldn't have to talk to a donkey! And I wouldn't have to fear robbers and breathe the dust of this miserable road the Romans refuse to fix. But as you can see, the road matches Matthias. It is a nothing road as I am a nothing man. A nothing that Peter wants to see. Quit nibbling that grass; it is time to go.

What can Peter want with me? Have I done something wrong again? I have tried my best, but as you know, Donkey, my best is a poor imitation of most people's worst. Do you remember, Donkey, when the Master sent us out and said, "There is too much harvest and too few

workers," or something like that. You see, I can't even remember important things like what the Master said. Matthias the Dull One, that's what you're thinking, isn't it? Well, you're right. The Master told us we would talk to people and my heart almost stopped. I, Matthias the No-body, was going to go to other towns and talk to people I had never met! Didn't the Master know I don't talk to people I don't know? I don't talk to people I DO know! I have never been able to talk to people. As you know—yes, I'm talking to you, Donkey!—I talk to animals. And rocks. And scrolls.

Did I tell you about that time one of the rabbis caught me talking back to the Job scroll? Can you imagine my embarrassment! I almost died. People were pointing at me and laughing. It was terrible! I tried to explain that I was reading and thinking at the same time, but the rabbi said I was drunk. Me, Matthias, who touches nothing. Nothing. Donkey, who knows better than you that I can only think when I talk... and not very well then.

Anyway, you remember that trip you and I made to that small village near Nablus? We were to talk—oh, I was frightened!—we were to talk to the people there and heal the sick. Heal the sick? Matthias the Nobody was supposed to walk up to a house and say, "Is anyone in there dying? I'm the great physician Matthias! Step aside, I'll heal him!"

Can you imagine what they would have said? "Yes, you must be a great physician because you rode up on that ignorant donkey"—excuse me, nothing personal—"and you smell terrible and your clothes are torn and you cannot look me in the eye." That's what they would have said, Donkey. I've been told—watch out for that chariot!—I said, I've been told it before. Why would this time be different?

I was terrified to talk to anyone, and I was ashamed of my clothing and my speech, which as you know—who should know better?—is slurred and unfit to be heard by anyone besides a Lycaonian donkey. I can only do jobs that keep me away from people. Why the Master allowed me to stay with him for all of those weeks and months I cannot understand. He spoke so well. His words were so strong, and people looked at him... oh, the way they looked at him! And Peter had the same great ability. In fact, all of the Twelve were natural leaders. I just wanted to crawl back in the shadows where they couldn't see me and listen to all of them teach. They could speak to anyone, anywhere, at any time. They were wonderful! But I... I could speak to no one. Who would listen to a nobody?

That was when the Master told us—told me—to leave our city and heal the sick and preach. Preach? You remember that was what he told me, but it was impossible. And you remember what happened, don't you, Donkey? I hung back. I hid, first behind a wall then behind a large hay cart. I couldn't force myself to do it!

Oh, of course, I found that little girl on the hay cart with a sprained wrist, and I fixed that, but that was nothing. I know, I know! Her father said the arm was broken, but it had to be only sprained. Even a nobody like me can fix a sprained wrist. But a broken wrist would have required a... miracle. Doesn't that prove it was only a sprain?

Why are you waggling your head, Donkey? Is there... oh, you mean that old man by the wall? Well, he was just sitting there with all those sores. I've told you that a dozen times. It was nothing. He was almost blind, and it looked as if no one had helped him for years, and I just did what the Master said and washed him... and sort of helped. And he got better.

Now, wait a minute, Donkey, that was not a miracle. It may have looked as if I healed him, and he did get better very quickly, but how many times have I told you that Matthias the Nobody cannot do miracles? It was just that some very odd things happened, and people got the wrong idea.

You want proof? Very well, I'll prove it to you. There was... there was ... all right, there was that widow who sat near her window all day long and mumbled things no one could understand. Her daughter said she had done that for months, since her husband was killed. You remember I began asking the widow very simple questions—what other kind would I ask?!—and within a few hours, two, three hours at the most, she stopped talking, looked at me, smiled and called my name. You see, that was no miracle! It was time for her to stop mumbling, that's all. Well, maybe talking to a nobody is useful, but a miracle... ?

Ooooooooh, Donkey. I failed... as I always fail. The Master told us to heal people, and I could not do it. I spent days and days in that small village until the people were as used to me as the town dog. I could never talk to them about healing. And as for preaching, I mentioned a few times to some beggars and travelers and what not that "The kingdom of God is near," and they seemed to listen, but that's not preaching like the rabbis do it. The only time they got excited was when I told them what the Master had been doing, and that he was coming to their village. Ah, Donkey, don't you remember how they smiled when I told them the Master's stories? But that wasn't preaching! I just told them what I saw. Don't bob your head like that, Donkey, and don't scrape my leg on that boulder. Matthias the Nobody cannot preach.

The Twelve... no, now it's the Eleven. Yes, Donkey, the Eleven can preach! If I could just be a mouse in the room where they meet, that's all I could ever want. I could listen to them for the rest of my life.

But I can't. I'm a nobody. And Matthias the Nobody has a summons from Peter, possibly the greatest of them all. I suppose he wants to tell me I have failed again.

In those days Peter stood up among the believers (a group numbering about one hundred and twenty) and said, "Brothers, the Scripture had to be fulfilled which the Holy Spirit spoke long ago through the mouth of David concerning Judas, who served as guide for those who arrested Jesus—he was one of our number and shared in this ministry.

"For," said Peter, "it is written in the book of Psalms,

'May his place be deserted;

let there be no one to dwell in it,' and,

'May another take his place of leadership.'

Therefore it is necessary to chose one of the men who have been with us the whole time the Lord Jesus went in and out among us, beginning from John's baptism to the time when Jesus was taken up from us. For one of these must become a witness with us of his resurrection."

So they proposed two men: Joseph called Barsabbas, also known as Justus, and Matthias. Then they prayed, "Lord, you know everyone's heart. Show us which of these two you have chosen to take over this apostolic ministry, which Judas left to go where he belongs." Then they drew lots, and the lot fell to Matthias; so he was added to the eleven apostles.

Acts 1:15-17, 20-26 [NIV]

THE OLD WARRIOR

9

Wisps of mist rose from the small pond in the cold pre-dawn darkness. Old Caleb plowed his blunt fingers through thick, gray hair and smiled, the lopsided grin crinkling the lines etching his leathery face. He remembered other mornings like this when the crisp quiet could disguise either a great discovery or sudden death. The memories were as crystalline as the dew wetting the door latch.

He laced on his heavy sandals, then moved quickly through the still-dark kitchen area. He snatched some day-old bread and a slab of cheese and stuffed it into his traveling sack. Unless his hunting was successful it would be all he would eat until sundown, which was fine with him. He had gone without food many times before; it would be a good experience to do it again. This city living was turning everyone in his family into pet rabbits. He grabbed a waterskin, then eased through the door and out into the brittle dawn.

Suddenly a middle-aged man leaned out of the window of the dilapidated house. Caleb dodged behind a stack of straw, but the man saw him and shouted, "Who's down there?" Elah, Old Caleb's oldest son, peered into the darkness. "Father, is that you? What are you doing up so early?"

"I'm going hunting."

"Father, come back to bed. You're too old to be out roaming at this time of night. You'll get sick from the night breezes."

"If you'll notice, it's less than an hour until sunrise. It wouldn't hurt you to get up and go hunting with me."

"I haven't got time to go hunting," Elah groaned. "I'm busy. Now, come on back to bed."

"Busy? You sit up there with your two brothers in that wreck of a house like pigeons with broken wings and coo to each other about how bad things are. Is that what keeps you busy?"

Elah, tall and thin, with a halo of frizzed hair, threw up his hands in frustration. "Just get back in the house."

"I can't. When I finish hunting I'm going on in to the village."

"The village?," Elah said quickly. "Why the village?"

"I'm going to call out the men—those that still have any courage at all!—and go up to Gilgal."

"Stay there!" Caleb heard Elah slam and bolt the window. A few seconds later Elah ran into the sheepfold, his nightdress flapping in the morning breeze. "What do you mean, you'll go to Gilgal?"

"That's a straight-forward statement. How many ways can it be understood? I plan to take some of the leaders of the village up to talk to Joshua about my inheritance."

"You can't do that! You can't go to Gilgal!"

Caleb leaned on a rainbarrel and peered at his scrawny, nervous forty-year-old son. "I walked over this land with Joshua and those ten mice who called themselves men. I walked around gathering those grapes and figs to show to our people. I walked and worked through the entire forty years in the wilderness, and I walked to this wreck of a house what seems like a life ago." Caleb's voice rose with the recitation. "What's so difficult about walking to the village? I can see it from here!"

"It's too far for someone your... age." Elah walked back and forth in the dusty yard. He shivered in the chill wind. "How many times have I told you that this is a difficult time for Israel, and you can't bother Joshua again. Things such as this take time. We've only been here five years."

"Only five years! No, to you it's only five years, but I've been on the march for forty-five years, since those cowards refused to follow Jehovah back at Kadesh Barnea. Because of them I'm not living on my land at Hebron." Old Caleb waved his fist and snorted out loud at the remembrance. "Those weaklings! It wasn't until later we found out we were traveling with field mice disguised as men! We were up beyond the Negev when we... "

"Stop living in the past, Father! Those days are gone. Look around you. If you throw a rock, you hit a Canaanite. They're all around us."

"All they have are swords. We have Jehovah."

Elah laughed, a short, angry snort. "And what about those sons of Anak the giant?"

"I'll fight the sons of Anak," Caleb said simply.

"You, Father? You're eighty-five!" Elah shivered again as a sharp wind swirled weeds around the sheepfold. "You just won't understand, will you? You're looking for the impossible. I wish you could remember what I told you."

"Oh, I remember! I hear it from every side, how this is not the time to do anything, that we have to be careful, that possibly someday we will have our inheritance at Hebron." Caleb's words poured out like vinegar. He spit in the dust in disgust. "I'm going to get my sword, gather some of the men from the city and get something done." He stalked toward the small, dilapidated house his entire family had been living in since the trip away from the desert. "In my day we would have gone in and taken what was ours. We weren't afraid of anything."

"But this isn't your day, Father. Can't you remember? You're eighty-five years old! Only Joshua is older. Your day passed years ago, when our families walked in the desert. I told you, we've decided you can't bother Joshua. And besides, we are in the land Jehovah promised us."

Old Caleb slammed his scarred fist on the rain barrel. "No! Some of the tribes have some of the land, but I was promised the pastureland around Hebron. Joshua promised it to me. Moses promised it to me. Jehovah promised it to ME! That's my land waiting out there. I want it, and I want it now." He spun toward the path leading to the village. "Well, the hunting can wait. I can still make a decision, and my decision is to find some men and take the land God promised me."

"Father! Stop it! You're too old to go around playing young men's games."

"Young men's games, is that what it's called now? You three little birdlets sit up in your dovecote and moan. That's certainly easier than taking what's yours. You and Iru and Naam are either too old or too young to fight, because you refuse to take what the Lord promised me, or have you forgotten that the pastures around Hebron will also belong to you?" Old Caleb's voice rang off the chipped plaster walls of the shabby house. "Look at this place! It's not mine, it's not yours, it's just a broken Caananite hovel. Did you fight for it? Of course not!" Caleb jammed a finger toward Hebron, still invisible in the blackness. "That's my land out there. And I've just decided I'm going to get it."

Elah blocked his way. "No, Father, you can't. We won't let you."

"We? And just who is this we in our conversation?"

"Three sons of an old man trying to play at being young. All of those stories about getting the grapes and figs, nobody believes those things anymore. If you want to tell the children your stories, that's fine, but don't tell them to us. And stay away from Gilgal. Leave the leading to your sons."

"Then lead!" Caleb backed away from his son. "I'm waiting for you to lead me to Hebron." He slapped his cloak impatiently. "You're not going anywhere, are you? You're going back to your two brothers and your friends and drink a bit of wine and whine about how cramped you are in this house and how your ancient father wants to do crazy things like take what's rightfully his. Am I right?"

Elah shouted toward the house where a light had just appeared. "Iru! Naam!" Almost immediately two men, one slight and squinting in the dim light, the other round as a pomegranate, ran into the weed-grown yard. "Tell your father what we decided yesterday."

Iru, the nearsighted one, peered into the darkness. "Father, we decided that—oh, you're over there!—we decided that it would only embarrass our families and disturb Joshua and the rest of the leaders if you went up to Gilgal. You... can't leave here." He backed away, sure of the coming explosion.

"Ah," Old Caleb said. "And how will you do that? Will you lock me in my room? Will I have a chain around my leg?"

"Of course not, Father!," Naam boomed, his fat body quivering with the effort. "We've just instructed the shepherds that you are to stay here, and we've blocked off the road to the village." He aimed his round stomach toward the kitchen area. "We won't stop you; they will. Come, let's have some food."

Caleb squinted at his sons, their three odd shapes moving nervously in the dim fingers of dawn. He started to speak, but instead he let his shoulders slump. He rubbed his eyes, then turned to trudge slowly out past the sheepfold. He was the image of a beaten old man. He turned once to look sadly at his sons, but they had already lost interest in him. "You will pen me up in this ugly Canaanite valley?," he muttered. He glanced up at the steep hill behind the sheepfold. "You will when the sun rises in the west!"

He leaped the small ravine stretching beside the hill and shoved his way through a stand of wild olive saplings. Within minutes he was high on the hill. Below, the first glints of the sun outlined the captured house and the gateless sheepfold where he and his sons and their families had lived for far too many frustrating months.

Caleb topped the hill and without a backward glance began a half-run, half-stumble down a faint trail he remembered from years before. It was on such a morning as this half a lifetime before that he walked these same hills and valleys. For forty days he and Joshua and those ten trembling mice scouted the land, until they found the huge clumps of grapes in what they came to call the Valley of Eschol, the Valley of Clusters. He snorted at the cowards who could not muster enough courage to give an honest report, who were afraid to take what Jehovah had given them.

With his knife he cut a terebinth sapling. He whittled as he strode the crude path through the hills toward Gilgal, and soon had a serviceable walking staff. He reached in his traveling sack, broke off a piece of cheese, then ate it with huge, smacking bites.

Far to the east the sun edged above the low hills surrounding Hebron. "Those are my pastures you're lighting, sun. Treat them well, and don't blister the grass. I will be there soon enough." He stretched his arms luxuriantly, swung the sapling staff at a gopher, and laughed loudly. God was good. His promises were there for the taking. It was wonderful to be alive!

Now the men of Judah approached Joshua at Gilgal, and Caleb son of Jephunneh the Kenizzite said to him, "You know what the Lord said to Moses the man of God at Kadesh Barnea about you and me. I was forty years old when Moses the servant of the Lord sent me from Kadesh Barnea to explore the land. And I brought him back a report according to my convictions, but my brothers who went up with me made the hearts of the people melt with fear. I, however, followed the Lord my God wholeheartedly. So on that day Moses swore to me, 'The land on which your feet have walked will be your inheritance and that of your children forever, because you have followed the Lord my God wholeheartedly.'

"Now then, just as the Lord promised, he has kept me alive for forty-five years since the time he said this to Moses, while Israel moved about in the desert. So here I am today, eighty-five years old! I am still as strong today as the day Moses sent me out; I'm just as vigorous to go out to battle now as I was then. Now give me this hill country that the Lord promised me that day. You yourself heard then that the Anakites were there and their cities were large and fortified, but, the Lord helping me, I will drive them out just as he said."

Then Joshua blessed Caleb son of Jephunneh and gave him Hebron as his inheritance. So Hebron has belonged to Caleb son of Jephunneh the Kenizzite ever since, because he followed the Lord, the God of Israel, wholeheartedly.

Joshua 14:6-14 [NIV]

THE MESSENGER

10

This day had been particularly unkind to Ananias. The slight, nervous man shook his head at the miserable change in his heretofore placid existence. A leak in his small cloth shop ruined an entire bolt of orange linen from Egypt. Then, two shrill women from his congregation wasted an hour complaining about some noisy children in the assembly. And finally, just before the noon meal, the Vision.

He swabbed his receding forehead with a scrap of cotton cloth as he remembered the tomb-like silence that preceeded the vision. For a change his cool, precisely-arranged shop was empty. He was at his favorite work, bent contentedly over an inventory of a shipment of wool which had just arrived from Persia. Suddenly, the hush covered him like a shroud. Even the scratch of his pen was lost in the echoless stillness. He looked up, startled at the strange quiet.

Carefully, with great precision, the Lord called Ananias by name, and like the dedicated God-fearer he was, Ananias answered. Or at least the Lord must have assumed his terrified gargle was an answer.

The next thing Ananias heard was the Lord telling him to go commit suicide. In truth, it wasn't as blatant as all that. What actually came out was an order for Ananias to go see someone named Judas on Straight Street—and ask if he had a guest from Tarsus.

Ananias gasped, then inquired softly concerning the given name of this Tarsian.

Dimly, he heard the word Saul.

Ananias trembled again at the name. Saul. The Madman of Tarsus. Oh, yes, he'd heard of him. Was there a soul, Christian or Jew, who hadn't heard the name?

Ananias wanted to explain to the Lord that bad news travels fast, and the current information about this particular Saul suggested that getting involved with him was about as intriguing as being hit by lightning. Ananias allowed as how there had already been enough damage to the saints down in Jerusalem, and now the street gossip had it that Saul was up here in Damascus to take any Christians he could find and slap them in chains.

The Lord went on to describe this Saul as blind and praying, and that he was going to...

Ananias interrupted to suggest that although it was to this Tarsian's credit that he had been praying, his history suggested that anyone getting in his way stood a fine chance of going to prison or worse. Much worse.

No, the Lord insisted that Saul had been told that a man named Ananias was going to come and put his hands on him and restore his sight. The Lord explained that this particular Saul was actually a chosen instrument of His to go out and preach to the Gentiles.

Ananias was nonplused at this information. He inferred, without actually suggesting the Lord might be inconsistent, that the words Gentile and chosen instrument appeared at first blush to be contradictory terms.

But the Lord assured Ananias that Saul was to carry His name before the Gentiles and their kings and before the people of Israel, and that Saul was going to be shown how much he would have to suffer for the name of the Lord.

And that was it. The street noises came back, a customer wandered in to look over some items, and Ananias was left to figure out how a shy, placid Jewish Christian got himself in this sort of mess. All he had to do was go tell a demented fanatic who hated Christians that it was time for him to start hurting. Oh, yes, that was certainly an attractive thought for a peaceful cloth seller!

Of course, the rest of the day was a disaster. What could he say to anyone? That he had seen a Vision of the Lord? Really, now! If he had made such a ridiculous statement he just knew anyone hearing that would look at him like a piece of three-day-old fish. The other person would certainly smile pityingly, then intimate something about Ananias working too hard in the sun or taking his duties at church too seriously or eating something a bit too old. Ananias knew he was totally wrong for the role of hero. His reed-thin body could hardly stand straight in a breeze; his skin was the color of bread dough from long hours spent inside tallying up his beloved figures; plus he always ran from any kind of confrontation. Always.

All afternoon his clerk kept squinting at Ananias, and even questioned him several times as to his general or specific health. The hint was obvious: Ananias, you're acting strangely. You're not the introverted, predictable man I work for.

A dozen times Ananias was on the verge of trying to explain about the vision and Saul and the terrifying order from the Lord. But the words never quite got to his trembling lips.

Ananias truly didn't need that sort of conflict. He knew he was an ordinary man, and, all in all, rather a pedestrian and unexciting human. Neither challenge nor bold defiance had a place in his vocabulary. He just wanted to be left alone with his inventories and tidy shelves in the quiet of his workshop. Although he worked long hours for his congregation, it was always in a simple, organizational way, out of the public eye. He prepared the room for their worship services. He gathered the materials for their agape feasts. True, he often gave cloth to the needy for clothing, but he was so shy his clerk always delivered the gift. Given his choice he would take the all-night vigil with some sick brother or sweep out after a service. As for carrying bad news to somebody like Saul... his mind turned to mud at the absurdity of the idea.

Naturally, his first conscious thought was that the Lord had made a tremendous mistake. Well, not exactly a mistake, mind you, just a slight error in turning into the wrong shop. Ananias knew another cloth seller over on the next street who was loud and brave and an obvious choice for delivering such a message. That's it, he got the wrong man!

No, Ananias remembered being called by name, and since he was the only Christian named Ananias any-where around Damascus, then...

His next thought was... Ananias, get yourself OUT of here! There had to be someplace where he could be as valuable as acting as a message boy in Damascus.

But he quickly reasoned that he was surely incor-rect in that. He recalled Jonah tried the same thing, and his trip didn't exactly turn into a weekend in the country. More like a weekend in a fish.

Ananias slapped his face and sighed. Very well, possibly... he could go to the house, shout through the window what he was supposed to say, and then run. No, that wouldn't work. The Lord said he had to place his hands on the man. On Saul the Madman! Ananias almost cried at the thought.

But slowly, painfully, Ananias realized that he would, in fact, be taking this assignment. He guessed he had always known he would take it. Since he never refused any commission given him if it concerned his small band of Christians, why should he think this one would be different?

But there were tremendous problems. For instance, Saul was educated and he had the backing of all of those important Jews, not to mention the high priests. How do you address such a man? Would he call him Brother? He's no believer... but the Lord said he was a chosen instrument. Now, wait a minute, the Lord also said he would carry the Lord's name before the Gentiles. The Gentiles? Ananias trembled at the very thought of having to get mixed up with them.

Ananias shook his head to clear it. He swabbed his face with another piece of cotton cloth.

All right, Ananias figured he could only die once. And it certainly would be an educational meeting. So... where was that? Oh, yes, Straight Street, and then ask for the house of somebody named Judas.

Well, all right...

Well, Ananias figured he should leave soon...

Well, when he was baptized no one promised he would have either a long or an unexciting life.

Well... all right.

In Damascus there was a disciple named Ananias. The Lord called to him in a vision, "Ananias!"

"Yes, Lord," he answered.

The Lord told him, "Go to the house of Judas on Straight Street and ask for a man from Tarsus named Saul, for he is praying. In a vision he has seen a man named Ananias come and place his hands on him to restore his sight."

"Lord," Ananias answered, "I have heard many reports about this man and all the harm he has done to your saints in Jerusalem. And he has come here with authority from the chief priests to arrest all who call on your name."

But the Lord said to Ananias, "Go! This man is my chosen instrument to carry my name before the Gentiles and their kings and before the people of Israel. I will show him how much he must suffer for my name."

Then Ananias went to the house and entered it. Placing his hands on Saul, he said, "Brother Saul, the Lord—Jesus, who appeared to you on the road as you were coming here—has sent me so that you may see again and be filled with the Holy Spirit." Immediately, something like scales fell from Saul's eyes, and he could see again. He got up and was baptized, and after taking some food, he re-gained his strength.

Acts 9:10-22 [NIV]

THE MAN BORN BLIND

11

His neighbors has never seen anything like it. For three days and nights Iram hadn't slept. Instead, he leaped and pranced across the hard-packed dirt in front of his parents' small house, picking up first a flower then a stone from the fence. He would gaze at the stone as fervently as the flower until he dropped both to run to a neighbor's house and call through the door. As soon as someone answered, he would quickly touch the neighbor's clothing or face or hands, laugh loudly and whirl to bounce and flail his arms in a heavy-footed dance down the street.

A neighbor woman, chubby and red-faced, called to a friend who had just dodged the leaping man. "You know, I liked him better before."

The spritely, bird-like second woman shook her head at Iram, who had just stopped a total stranger to ask him something. "I just don't understand what happened. For almost twenty-five years Iram was blind, then last Sabbath he came running and screaming that he could see." The frail woman squinted at Iram's prancing around the stranger. "What happened?"

"What happened? What happened?! Are you deaf that you haven't heard that story twenty times or a hundred? Iram cries and laughs and blubbers his way through that whole strange tale for anyone who will stand still." The heavy woman flapped her hands in frustration. "No one in my house has had a decent night's sleep since whatever happened... happened. He pounds on my door in the middle of the night to ask a question or to talk or just to watch me get angry! I yell at him, my husband threatens him, my children are crying, but he just bleats out that cackling laugh and runs back into the street to bother someone else. He told me—well, actually he yelled at me— that he's afraid if he closes his eyes, they'll never open again. And just this morning he... look out! Here he comes again!"

The two women dodged behind a low fence as Iram the Blind Man skidded around the corner of a house, tumbled laughing into a bush, then lay open-mouthed at a flock of small birds swooping and cutting. Then he saw the women.

"Look! Those are birds, aren't they?" He waved both hands violently as he pointed and shouted, then he looked at his waving hands and laughed. "Of course, I've heard of them, but just look how they move, like my arms." He jumped up and down, making the ragged sleeves of his beggar's cloak flap. "Or like these sleeves! Or like... who's that?" He pointed at a small, hunched man walking stiffly on the other side of the dusty street. "Why is he waving?"

The slight woman peered into the sunshine. "It's our rabbi. I think he wants you, Iram."

"Wonderful! And I want to see him. I've never seen him before, you know!" Immediately he leaped across the low fence and lurched into the cobblestoned street. "Rabbi ben-Isaac! Is this what you look like? You sounded so much taller in synagogue."

"Is that truly you, Iram?" The old man squinted through bleary eyes at the nervous young man. "I mean, you are actually Iram the blind man, the son of Hashim the sandal-maker?"

"Yes. Yes! But now I should be called Iram the Formerly Blind Man, because I can see. And I can run!" Iram leaped in the air and capered back and forth in the narrow street. "And I am really taller than you, Rabbi ben-Isaac. Among other things, that was one thing I didn't know."

"Well, something I don't know is how you could be blind last Sabbath morning, but by Sabbath noon you could see. Can you explain that?"

"Absolutely! This other rabbi came by and put some mud on my eyes, and then he told me to go to Siloam and wash it off. So I stumbled and crawled to the pool, and when I finally got there and did what he told me, suddenly the sun splashed in my eyes. I could see!"

Rabbi ben-Isaac bent closer to peer at the bright eyes of the young man. "Yes, I suppose you are Iram the beggar." He shook his head slowly as he frowned. "And that means I have to take you to some of our other leaders."

"Wonderful! Where are they, on the other side of our village? I hope so, since I've only been there once since the miracle."

"Don't say that word!," ben-Isaac hissed. "No one has certified that it's a genuine miracle, so we can't call it that. That's why I'm taking you to... "

"Not a miracle?! What are you saying? For twenty-five years and more I lived in blackness much worse than the three nights since my mira... since my healing. And now, I can see everything. And I want to see everything! Did you know the moon disappears in the daytime? Now, I call that a miracle! Let's go see the leaders. Who are they?"

"A delegation of the Pharisees has requested that you come see them."

"Marvelous! I've always wondered what they were like, those people who talk so bravely. Of course, I had to listen through the window at synagogue because no one wanted me in the assembly. Are they very tall?"

"Look for yourself. They're coming toward us."

Iram the Formerly Blind Man stopped dead. "Those are Pharisees? But they're just like you... and me. Are you sure those are Pharisees? I thought they were big and important."

"Big, no. Important, yes," Rabbi ben-Isaac whispered. "Now, just stand here and let them speak first. They have some questions for you."

"Oh, this is wonderful! And I have some questions for them!"

"No!," ben-Isaac moaned, his eyes squinting at the trouble about to occur. "You don't question them, they question you. Iram, just listen. Then—we'll see." The rabbi held up one hand in greeting. "Issicar! Nebai! Over here."

The two men, dressed identically in flowing white robes, peered with unsmiling eyes at the ragged, grinning man in front of them. Prominent decorations stated plainly that they were leaders of the conservative sect called the Pharisees. The taller one, named Issicar, pressed his fingertips together, then spoke slowly. "Are you Iram the beggar? The blind beggar?"

"Actually, I prefer to be called Iram the Formerly Blind Beggar. It has a very nice sound, don't you... "

"How can you be 'formerly' blind?"

"It was the miracle! For twenty-five years I saw nothing, and now... "

"There was no miracle!" Nebai, bald as a metal bowl and with a body shaped like a melon, grabbed Iram by his shoulders. "There was no miracle."

Iram shrugged elaborately, then cackled at the look on the two men's faces. "Call it what you want, but for twenty-five years I couldn't see, and now I can see. What do you suppose would be the number of blind beggars who are healed when they are twenty-five? One out of every twelve? Possibly one out of every hundred?" He grinned slyly. "Or am I the first? Calling it something besides a miracle may be difficult for the people who have seen me."

"Iram," the taller, haughty Pharisee snarled, "it will not be you who will make these decisions. Stand still! And quit looking at that camel."

"Is that what that is?," Iram exclaimed. "I had no idea God made so many different kinds of things. And they are there just for our looking! What a wonderful world!"

"Who did this evil thing to you?"

"What evil? Where?" Iram looked around, startled. "Oh, you mean my eyes. That was Rabbi Jesus."

"He's no rabbi," Nebai snickered, "he's just a wandering fake."

Iram jabbed his forefingers toward his own eyes. "These are not fake eyes."

"No," Issicar said carefully, "they are sinful eyes. Sin caused your blindness. That's a well known fact. Everyone knows that."

"Not so! Not so. According to Rabbi Jesus neither my parents nor I sinned to cause me to be born blind." Iram folded his arms and smiled broadly as he watched a mother cat carry her kittens.

Issicar lowered his eyelids craftily. "And what do you have to say about this Jesus, this wandering false teacher?"

"Obviously he's a prophet."

"Aha! Do you know that for that statement alone we could put you out of the synagogue meeting. You know this Jesus must be a sinner. He did—whatever he did—on the sabbath. Tell us again how he did—whatever he did."

Iram pointed his finger first at one then the other of the Pharisees. "Ooooooh, I see! You want to know about him so you can study with him. That's it, isn't it?"

Issicar's reed-thin body tensed and straightened. "We follow Moses. We don't know who this Jesus is. He comes from no prominent family, he studied with no great teacher, he's a nothing and a nobody." He turned to look at Nebai's round head bobbing vigorously.

"And still," Iram said carefully, "I was blind but now I can see."

Issicar flapped some dust from his robes as he sighed elaborately. "It's plain that you cannot be taught what is right. Then," he paused dramatically for the benefit of the crowd which had gathered, "to help you learn, from now on, you will not be allowed in our synagogue. You are no longer part of our community. You started life in sin, and you will have to live in that sin. Come, Nebai. We must leave this sinner." The two white-robed men backed up carefully, then turned and walked away.

Slowly the crowd surrounding Iram dissolved. The people looked away, afraid of meeting Iram's confused glances. Suddenly, with a burst of insight as brilliant as his first glimple of sunlight, Iram understood what he had been avoiding since last Sabbath: everything he had known up to this point would be changed. He could never again simply sit and beg as he had before, his sightless eyes and open palm turned upward. His parents would no longer take care of him as they had for his entire life. He had to find some kind of work that would support him. Within three days he had what was never his: responsibility. And more profound than that, he now had the opportunity to fail.

Iram wanted to leap up and run thoughtlessly through the village as he had for the past three days, but a great wave of weariness washed over him. He almost wished for the return of his blindness so he could take his old, comfortable seat by the town well. There were no problems at the well, only a cry for alms and waiting for the small coins that were sure to come. Iram sighed as he dropped onto some grass in the shade of a tall sycamore.

Then a movement caught his eye. An infant, a chubby boy chasing a grasshopper, toddled around a corner, looked up at him—and laughed. The delighted gurgle was close to the way Iram had been laughing for the past three days whenever he saw something new and startling.

Slowly, a broad smile spread across Iram's face. "That's it! I'm like that child," he cried. "For me everything is new. I'm no longer limited to my spot near our village well. I can see the world."

Then he frowned again. "But just the memory of blackness is no great comfort. What can I take with me to keep me from being lonely? I can't beg, and even if I tried, the other beggars would hate me." He shivered at the sudden chill of loneliness.

Then a shadow fell over Iram. He glanced up at a man of medium height in nondescript clothes who stood looking at him. A smile as gentle as a child's touch told Iram he had nothing to fear. Ever.

Jesus heard that they had thrown him out, and when he found him, he said, "Do you believe in the Son of Man?"

"Who is he, sir?" the man asked. "Tell me so that I may believe in him."

Jesus said, "You have now seen him; in fact, he is the one speaking with you."

Then the man said, "Lord, I believe," and he worshiped him.

John 9:1-41 [NIV]

THE MAKER OF SONGS

12

The Pilgrim squinted against the thunder of the water gushing through split boulders near the base of Mount Hermon. As his dark eyes gazed up toward the crags hiding the source of the powerful mountain stream a song his Grandfather taught him rushed to his lips. He alternately clapped his hands and snapped his fingers to accompany the lines learned in childhood:

> Deep calls to deep
>> in the roar of your waterfalls;
> all your waves and breakers
>> have swept over me.

The young man's sundarkened face remained tilted upward, his voice almost lost against the brawling water's noise. Far above he saw the snows which birthed

the watercourse. He raised his arms as if in benediction for the mist drifting down to cool him and for the tiny rainbows formed where the water spewed through a crevice. But most of all he gave thanks for the songs of his dead Grandfather. Without them he knew he would be half-mute. "Grandfather," he said aloud to the boulders and river thicket, "you would be happy here. This mountain is worthy of your songs."

Then he looked longingly to the south, past the Sea of Galilee and Mount Gilboa, toward Jerusalem. As if in benediction, a cool breeze dropped off the mountain, parting his thick, black hair. He smiled as he breathed deeply. Finally, the journey I promised my Grandfather is half finished!

He called himself a Maker of Songs. He had long ago determined that his work would be the singing of the songs his Grandfather taught him and the writing of new ones. If he could make it to the Temple his songs would finally form out of those wandering, disjointed words and phrases that swam through his own heart. For years, tiny slivers of sentences flickered through his mind but, like dew-frost, they defied holding and examining.

In his most honest moments he knew his Grandfather's songs dominated his singing. Always a sentence from one of his Grandfather's songs floated up to explain a situation or comfort a hurt. But now... now he was on his way to Jerusalem. To see the Temple! And find his own song.

The Temple! He sucked in his breath at the thought. He knew every doorway and window in the great Temple at Jerusalem as if he had been born there. That's how thoroughly his Grandfather had coached him. The Temple had formed the centerpiece of his Grandfather's memories after he had been carried off by the soldiers of the Assyrian king. Only the songs and the image of the Temple were left to comfort the old man. But now he was dead, and it was time to take the songs home. Home to the Temple.

These thoughts dominated the young Pilgrim so thoroughly that the days of his journey passed as minutes. He was less than half a day's walk to Jerusalem, and concentrating so completely on two phrases of his own that he failed to see the thick bush at the base of a small hill.

"You, Hebrew." The coarse voice startled the Pilgrim. "Yes, you with that band around your head. Come here." A filthy camel driver, tall, with a grease-stained beard, walked out from behind the bush. He pointed toward the young Pilgrim.

"What do you want?" the Pilgrim asked warily. He backed up a step.

"Stand still, you scrawny Jew. What are you doing out here, walking by yourself?"

"I'm—on my way to Jerusalem."

"From the looks of your clothes you obviously don't have any money. What's in that leather pouch you're carrying?"

The young man dug out a small bit of cheese. "Just the last of my food."

"Why are you going to Jerusalem?"

"To see the Temple. I promised my Grandfather I would see it for him."

"And then what?" The man smirked as he motioned with his hand.

The Pilgrim knew what was coming. He began edging away. "I will just—look at it." Another camel driver leaped from behind the bush and laughed as he grabbed a stone. The Pilgrim backed away, then broke and ran when the two ragged caravaniers hurled curses and rocks at him. He ran till his breath came in short, painful bursts. Finally he slowed and looked back at the two men laughing and slapping their legs at the crazy Hebrew walking by himself.

He had played that scene many times before. As a musician he had sung his songs for banquets and then, being small, had often been thrown out without being paid. Sometimes he had performed in taverns only to be laughed at and doused with garbage when he asked for his fee. But it wasn't too bad, he thought. He had been paid often enough to buy food and an occasional new pair of sandals. And always there were the songs from his Grandfather and the hope of seeing the Temple. He picked up two flat stones and tapped them together in rhythm to the refrain of an old song his Grandfather often sang at sundown.

Why are you downcast, O my soul?

Why so disturbed within me?

Put your hope in God,

for I will yet praise him,

my Savior and my God.

The dusty road turned abruptly near the crest of the hill he had been climbing, and suddenly in the distance, less than an hour away, the walls of Jerusalem jutted up to dominate the entire valley. He sucked in his breath at the immensity of the stones laying course on course. And there, the top barely visible, was the Temple. After all of those years and those songs...

He fell in with a small group of farmers bringing vegetables to the market. He wanted to cry out at the beauty of the Temple, to ask these citizens if they had been changed by constantly seeing its elegance and grace. But they were engrossed in their own laughing and complaining, and were oblivious to the Temple's glory. Finally, he edged through the thick door of the Fish Gate where he fell back against the stone wall in amazement at his first clear sight of the Temple of Solomon.

He dropped to his knees. His fingers poked through some rubble until they closed on a stick and a broken jar. Slowly, almost inaudibly, he began beating a slow rhythm on the fired clay shard. He closed his eyes and began his search for some words to describe his love for the building.

But something was wrong. Not only would the words not form, but even the melody he made tasted like vinegar. He opened his eyes to stare at the Temple.

He beat the stick harder against the broken jar, the jagged rhythm ringing in the afternoon heat. Still no melody appeared.

He looked up into the curious stares of a few merchants and farmers. "What's that foreigner muttering about," someone said. "It's just another drunken musician," he heard a man snort.

The Pilgrim could only lean his head against the cool stone of the fortress walls. Where were his Temple words, the ones he stored up against this moment? He had come all this way to see this Temple of God, and his heart had turned into a knot of wood. Where was the song he had dreamed about?

He rolled to his knees, then stood slowly. He walked to his left around the Temple, feeling for more words, more phrases that would describe his years of longing for... what? Suddenly his head felt light, as if he were coming out of a dream. As he turned to gaze up at the finely cut stone traceries, at the carved limestone lintels and the smooth facings of the windows, suddenly he knew. He had waited all these years for... for... for his Grandfather's memories!

That was it. The memories were not his. His Grandfather had prepared him for the Temple, but what his Grandfather could never give the young man were the memories of the attack of the Assyrian soldiers, the terror of being chained and led away from God's Temple, the years of being left in a foreign land with only dimming images and old songs. His Grandfather had given him the Temple of the Lord, which had sustained the old man. What the young Maker of Songs needed was the Lord of the Temple. He needed the Occupant, not the structure.

Slowly, as if it were a mist evaporating, his eyes saw through stacked stones of the Temple. He knew now it was never the stone building he searched for, it was the creator of the stone and the creator of the stone mason. The Pilgrim staggered back at his realization that the Temple, despite its beauty, would someday crumble. But the God of the Temple would live forever.

With this thought cleansing his mind like a spring rain, the young Pilgrim opened his mouth. The vision of his song, as brilliant and clear as a new dawn, glowed bright and pure. He lifted his face toward the sky and began a slow shuffling dance of joy. Within seconds the words began flowing effortlessly and pure like warm honey.

> *How lovely is your dwelling place, O Lord Almighty!*
>
> *My soul yearns, even faints for the courts of the Lord;*
>
> *my heart and my flesh cry out for the living God.*

There it was! The Pilgrim's voice opened and a melody poured out, a song boiling from his very soul. The passersby stopped to listen, and as he repeated the words they nodded and smiled. Someone, a child perhaps, said, "Sing it again." The Pilgrim smiled as the tears rolled down his cheeks. His clapping hands led the people surrounding him:

> *Blessed are those whose strength is in you,*
>
> *who have set their hearts on pilgrimage.*

The sun glistened on the formed stone of the Temple, but the Maker of Songs couldn't see it. He only saw the people singing his song. He had found his voice. He was home.

How lovely is your dwelling place, O Lord Almighty!

My soul yearns, even faints for the courts of the Lord;

my heart and my flesh cry out for the living God.

Even the sparrow has found a home,

and the swallow a nest for herself, where she may have her young—

a place near your altar, O Lord Almighty, my King and my God.

Blessed are those who dwell in your house; they are ever praising you.

Blessed are those whose strength is in you,

who have set their hearts on pilgrimage.

As they pass through the Valley of Baca, they make it a place of springs;

the autumn rains also cover it with pools.

They go from strength to strength till each appears before God in Zion.

Hear my prayer, O Lord God Almighty; listen to me, O God of Jacob.

Look upon our shield, O God; look with favor on your
anointed one.

Better is one day in your courts than a thousand elsewhere;

    I would rather be a doorkeeper in the house of my God

        than dwell in the tents of the wicked.

For the Lord God is a sun and shield; the Lord bestows favor
and honor;

    no good thing does he withold from those whose walk
    is blameless.

O Lord Almighty, blessed is the man who trusts in you.

    Psalm 84 [NIV]